RECIPES THAT WORK

Kevin Dundon

RECIPES THAT WORK

More than 120
easy recipes for
delicious food

Kevin Dundon

Collins

Dedication

To my three wonderful children: Emily, Sophie and Tom

First published in 2011 by Collins
an imprint of HarperCollins*Publishers*
77–85 Fulham Palace Road
London W6 8JB

www.harpercollins.co.uk

10 9 8 7 6 5 4 3 2 1

Photography © Martin Poole 2011
Text © Kevin Dundon 2011

A catalogue record for this book is available from the British Library.

ISBN: 978-0-00-738303-0

Layout by Sophie Martin
Colour reproduction by Saxon, printing and binding by South China

Contents

INTRODUCTION

Nowadays people lead such busy lives, so when they select a new recipe to cook for their family or friends, they want it to work perfectly and without fail, the first time and every time. The recipes in this book do just that.

It's a collection of tried-and-tested recipes that I have built up over my years in the food industry. I have worked in many different places and kitchens, and I have used all of my experience and knowledge to write this book.

The face of food has changed a lot since I first became a chef. Right now, home-cooked comfort food is the theme that is very much in vogue. People love to be able to visit their local butchers and supermarkets, to bring home their produce and cook up a fantastic meal from scratch for their nearest and dearest.

In *Recipes that Work* I have tried to use everyday ingredients that you're bound to have at home, but I've also jazzed them up a little with plenty of added twists. I hope that you enjoy cooking and eating your way through my recipes.

CHAPTER I
SOUPS

A bowl of soup is perhaps the most nourishing meal you can have. I remember coming in from school as a child, when Mum would always have some homemade soup and brown bread ready for us, especially in the winter. It would keep us all going until our evening meal.

All these years later, soup is one of my favourite lunchtime snacks. A bowl of delicious soup will give you plenty of energy for the day. We always have homemade soup in the fridge at home and my children love it. Just like my mother used to do, now I find myself serving it up to them when they get home from school. Soup can also be a welcome gift to take over to a friend's house.

In this chapter I have tried to give you recipes for a variety of styles – some are creamy soups and others are chunky broths. The most important thing to remember about soup is not to overcook it. You must use the freshest of vegetables and just cook them lightly with a little seasoning for a delicious, flavoursome meal.

ROASTED VEGETABLE SOUP

―――――

This is a warming, nourishing soup that is perfect for a cold winter's day. The mild spices give it a really unusual flavour.

SERVES 6

1 sweet potato, peeled and chopped

2 medium carrots, peeled and chopped

300g/11oz butternut squash or turnip or broccoli or pumpkin or a mix, peeled, deseeded and chopped

2 celery sticks, chopped

1 medium leek, trimmed and chopped

½ medium onion, peeled and chopped

2.5cm/1in piece fresh root ginger (gingerroot), peeled and chopped

3 garlic cloves, peeled and chopped

50g/2oz/½ stick butter

2 large fresh thyme sprigs

1.25 litres/2 pints/5 cups chicken or vegetable stock (see pages 203–4)

150ml/5fl oz/⅔ cup pouring cream

A pinch of ground cinnamon, plus extra to garnish (optional)

Salt and freshly ground black pepper

Crème fraîche or pouring cream, to garnish

1 Place the sweet potato, carrots, butternut squash, celery, leek, onion, ginger and garlic in a large bowl.

2 Heat a large saucepan with the butter, toss in all the vegetables together with the thyme sprigs and cook gently over a low heat and without colouring for 8–10 minutes or until the smaller vegetables are beginning to soften.

3 Next add about two-thirds of the stock and bring the mixture to a slow boil. Reduce the heat and simmer for a further 15–20 minutes or until all of the vegetables have softened down completely.

4 Remove the pan from the heat and, using a hand-held electric blender, blitz the soup until it is nice and smooth. Mix in the cream and ground cinnamon at this stage then return to the heat and bring back to a very gentle boil. If you would like a thinner soup, now would be the best time to add some additional stock to thin it down. Taste and adjust the seasoning.

5 Transfer the soup to serving bowls or cups and garnish with a little crème fraîche or pouring cream infused with some additional ground cinnamon. Serve as required or allow the soup to cool then transfer to suitable containers and freeze for up to 2 months.

CAULIFLOWER AND BLUE CHEESE SOUP

This is a classic combination of flavours. It is quite a filling soup and a little goes a long way. Try adding some curry powder during cooking for a mild spiced alternative.

SERVES 6–8

50g/2oz/½ stick butter

I large onion, peeled and chopped into large chunks

I large leek, trimmed and chopped into large chunks

3 garlic cloves, peeled and crushed

2 bay leaves

I large potato, peeled and chopped into large chunks

I large head cauliflower, chopped into large chunks

Salt and freshly ground black pepper

1.25 litres/2 pints/5 cups well-flavoured chicken or vegetable stock (see pages 203–4), warmed

300ml/10fl oz/1¼ cups pouring cream

150g/5oz blue cheese, plus extra to garnish

I Melt the butter in a large saucepan, add the onion, leeks and garlic and sweat over a low heat for about 6–8 minutes until the vegetables have softened. Add the bay leaves and chopped potato and cauliflower and sweat them for another moment or two. Season lightly with salt and pepper.

2 Next pour in the warmed stock and the cream and bring to the boil. Continue to boil for about 2–3 minutes then reduce the heat to a gentle simmer and simmer for a further 10–15 minutes until the vegetables have softened. Remove and discard the bay leaves.

3 Remove the pan from the heat and stir in half the blue cheese. Using a hand-held electric blender, blitz the soup, adding additional stock if you desire. Some people prefer a thicker or thinner soup. Taste and adjust the seasoning then reheat it gently.

4 Serve the soup garnished with the rest of the crumbled blue cheese on top.

ROASTED RED PEPPER AND TOMATO SOUP

———————

The colour of this soup is so inviting and it is a great way to use up the glut of early autumn tomatoes.

SERVES 6–8

3 medium red (bell) peppers

2 tbsp olive oil, plus extra for drizzling

Salt and freshly ground black pepper

1 small onion, peeled and finely chopped

2 garlic cloves, peeled and finely chopped

1kg/2lb 4oz ripe plum tomatoes, halved

700ml/1¼ pints/3 cups chicken or vegetable stock (see pages 203–4) or water

A pinch of brown sugar (optional)

100ml/3½fl oz/scant ½ cup pouring cream

TO GARNISH

Crème fraîche

Snipped fresh chives

1 Preheat the oven to 190°C (375°F), Gas mark 5.

2 Arrange the peppers on a baking tray and drizzle lightly with olive oil. Season with a little salt and pepper and roast in the oven for about 25 minutes until they are very soft and the skin is blistered. Put the peppers into a large bowl and cover tightly with clingfilm (plastic wrap), which will allow the skins to peel away easily. Leave until cool enough to handle, then peel away the skins, deseed and chop the roasted flesh roughly.

3 Heat the olive oil in a pan over a medium–high heat. Add the onion and garlic and sauté for a few minutes until golden. Add the tomatoes and continue to sauté for a further 5 minutes or so, until well heated through and just beginning to break down. Add the chopped peppers at this stage. Stir in the stock or water and bring to the boil. Reduce the heat and simmer for 15–20 minutes or until all the vegetables have softened completely.

4 Remove the pan from the heat and, using a hand-held electric blender, blitz to a smooth purée. Season to taste and add the sugar if you think the soup needs it. Sometimes the pepper can cause the soup to be a little bitter.

5 To serve, add the cream to the soup then return the pan to the heat and bring to the boil. Season to taste and ladle into warmed serving bowls. Garnish each bowl with a small dollop of crème fraîche and a sprinkling of chives.

SPICED PUMPKIN SOUP

———————

Pumpkin tends to be quite bland, so it often needs the addition of some spices to liven it up a little. This recipe will let you make use of all the flesh that gets scooped out when you're making Halloween decorations!

SERVES 6–8

50g/2oz/½ stick butter

2 carrots, peeled and chopped into large chunks

1 large potato or sweet potato, peeled and chopped into large chunks

1 leek, trimmed and chopped into large chunks

2 celery sticks, chopped into large chunks

900g/2lb pumpkin flesh, chopped into large chunks

½ medium onion, peeled and chopped into large chunks

3 garlic cloves, peeled and chopped

Salt and freshly ground black pepper

1 tsp curry paste or a pinch of crushed dried chilli flakes or 1 fresh chilli, finely chopped

75ml/3fl oz/⅓ cup pouring cream

1.25 litres/2 pints/5 cups chicken or vegetable stock (see pages 203–4)

TO GARNISH

About 1 tbsp crème fraîche

About ½ tbsp pumpkin seeds, toasted

1 Slowly melt the butter in a large saucepan, add the vegetables and garlic and mix thoroughly, then pan-roast over a medium heat for 6–8 minutes, stirring occasionally to prevent them sticking to the pan.

2 Season lightly at this stage then add the curry paste or chilli and allow to infuse with the vegetables.

3 Next add the cream and two-thirds of the stock. It is best to add just this amount of stock now, as it allows you to adjust or correct the consistency more accurately before serving. Bring to the boil then reduce the heat to a constant simmer and simmer for 15–20 minutes or until all of the vegetables have softened.

4 Remove the pan from the heat and, using a hand-held electric blender, blitz the soup until smooth, adjusting the consistency with the remaining stock as required. Taste and adjust the seasoning accordingly. For those that are more daring, you may wish to add extra chilli flakes.

5 Divide the soup either among little mini pumpkins, out of which you have scooped all the flesh, or teacups and saucers. Garnish with a little crème fraîche and toasted pumpkin seeds and serve.

TIP

This is a basic soup recipe, which you can vary depending on what you like. Try substituting the pumpkin for carrot and ginger, butternut squash, sweet potatoes, or parsnips.

CREAMY MUSHROOM AND THYME SOUP

Mushroom soup is a classic, but this version is particularly fabulous as the thyme adds a real edge. It's a recipe that can be made ahead of time and then just reheated as required. I normally use two-thirds button (white) mushrooms in this soup and one-third wild mushrooms, as the wild mushrooms are much more expensive.

SERVES 6–8

900g/2lb selection of mushrooms (mixture of button/white and wild), sliced

2 garlic cloves, peeled and roughly chopped

4–5 fresh thyme sprigs

50g/2oz/½ stick butter

1 leek, trimmed and roughly chopped

2 celery sticks, roughly chopped

1 large onion, peeled and roughly chopped

50g/2oz/⅓ cup plain (all-purpose) flour

1.25 litres/2 pints/5 cups boiling chicken or vegetable stock (see pages 203–4)

Salt and freshly ground black pepper

300ml/10fl oz/1¼ cups pouring cream

2 tsp truffle oil (optional; it has a very intense flavour)

Crème fraîche, to garnish

1 Preheat the oven to 160°C (325°F), Gas mark 3.

2 Place the mushrooms in a roasting tray with the garlic and thyme sprigs. Roast in the oven for 15–20 minutes or until just becoming tender but shrivelled up a little. This helps to develop and intensify their flavour. Keep a small amount of these roasted mushrooms aside to garnish the soup just before serving.

3 Melt the butter in a large saucepan, add the remaining vegetables and sauté gently for 4–5 minutes. Add the roasted mushrooms and sauté for a further 2–3 minutes. Add the flour and stir until the vegetables are coated and any liquid in the pan has dried up. This will act as a thickening agent.

4 Carefully pour in the boiling stock and bring to the boil. Reduce to a low simmer and simmer until the vegetables are all tender.

5 Remove the pan from the heat and season to taste. Add the cream and truffle oil, if using, then using a hand-held electric blender, blitz until smooth. Alternatively, use a food processor.

6 Serve the soup immediately or leave to reheat gently later. To garnish, add a spoonful of crème fraîche on the top and a little of the reserved roasted mushroom selection.

FRENCH ONION SOUP

This classic soup is very simple to make and, if you get it right, your family and friends will love it. It's just as good reheated the following day. The soup is traditionally made with beef stock but it can be made with vegetable stock if you are vegetarian.

SERVES 6

50g/2oz/½ stick butter

4 large onions, peeled and thinly sliced

3 garlic cloves, peeled and crushed

2-3 fresh thyme sprigs

2 tsp brown sugar

50g/2oz/⅓ cup plain (all-purpose) flour

½ glass red wine

1 litre/1¾ pints/4 cups good-quality hot beef stock (see page 202)

Salt and freshly ground black pepper

CROUTONS

1 French stick

50g/2oz/½ cup freshly grated Parmesan or Gruyère cheese

1 Melt the butter in a large saucepan. Carefully add the onions, garlic, thyme sprigs and sugar and sweat over a medium heat for about 10 minutes or until the onions have partially softened.

2 Next add the flour all in one go and stir until the onions are coated and any liquid in the pan has dried up. Pour in the red wine, which will immediately begin to thicken as it reacts with the flour, then gradually add the hot stock, stirring continuously. Season to taste with salt and pepper. Reduce the heat to low and simmer for about 45 minutes or until the onions are soft and the soup is well flavoured.

3 Meanwhile, preheat the grill or if using the oven preheat to 190°C (375°F) Gas mark 5.

4 Cut the French stick into slices about 1cm/½in thick and sprinkle with the grated cheese. Grill or bake in the oven until the cheese is melted and the bread is crispy.

5 Serve the croûtons on top of the fragrant soup and sprinkle with a few thyme leaves.

VICHYSSOISE

This is a leek and potato soup that is enriched with cream, chilled and puréed, and sprinkled with chives. It's a marriage of flavours made in heaven. It is important to include the sieving (straining); in fact, it may be necessary to do it twice to achieve the perfect smoothness.

SERVES 6–8

50g/2oz/½ stick unsalted butter

350g/12oz small leeks, trimmed and finely chopped

1 onion, peeled and finely chopped

225g/8oz potatoes, peeled and diced

1 celery stick, diced

1 garlic clove, peeled and crushed

Salt and freshly ground pepper

900ml/1½ pints/3½ cups chicken or vegetable stock (see pages 203–4)

150ml/5fl oz/⅔ cup milk

150ml/5fl oz/⅔ cup double (heavy) cream

Snipped fresh chives, to garnish

1 Melt the butter in a large heavy-based saucepan. As soon as it foams, stir in the leeks, onion, potatoes and celery until well coated. Add the garlic and season generously, then place a parchment paper circle directly on top of the vegetables to keep in the steam. Cover the pan with a tight-fitting lid and sweat over a low heat for about 10 minutes until the vegetables are soft and just beginning to colour.

2 Remove the lid and paper from the pan and pour in the stock. Bring to the boil and simmer for about 5 minutes or until the potatoes are completely tender. Transfer to a food processor and blitz in batches until smooth. Or use a hand-held electric blender.

3 Pass the soup through a fine sieve (strainer) set over a bowl (you may need to do this twice) and then pour into a clean pan. Season to taste then stir in the milk and most of the cream, reserving some for the garnish.

4 Reheat the soup gently, then ladle into a large bowl, cover with clingfilm (plastic wrap) and chill for at least 4 hours, or overnight, which is best.

5 To serve, ladle the vichyssoise into serving bowls and swirl in the reserved cream. Garnish with the chives and serve ice cold.

VARIATIONS

• Of course, this soup can also be served hot, garnished with crumbled Roquefort cheese for a special treat.

• For a richer version, replace the milk with cream or experiment with the proportion of leek to onion and potato, by adding some celeriac (celery root). I have even made it using cauliflower instead.

CURRIED PARSNIP
AND APPLE SOUP

This soup is one of my personal favourites. It has a smooth texture in the mouth but gives a sharp kick to the back of your throat. You can leave the parsnips a little chunky, as they do tend to cook down and disintegrate more easily than the other ingredients. If you or any of your guests are vegetarian, use vegetable stock and make sure the Thai green curry paste doesn't contain shrimp paste.

SERVES 6–8

25g/1oz/¼ stick butter

1 leek, trimmed and chopped roughly into chunks

2 celery sticks, chopped roughly into chunks

½ medium onion, peeled and chopped roughly into chunks

2 potatoes, peeled and chopped roughly into chunks

350g/12oz parsnips, peeled and chopped roughly into chunks

1 large cooking apple, peeled, cored and diced

2 level tsp Thai green curry paste

1.25 litres/2 pints/5 cups chicken or vegetable stock (see pages 203–4)

75ml/3fl oz/⅓ cup pouring cream

Salt and freshly ground black pepper

1 Melt the butter in a large saucepan, add the leek, celery, onion, potatoes, parsnips and apple and sauté for a few minutes until they are golden brown and beginning to soften.

2 Next add the Thai curry paste and stir into the vegetables then add a mixture of stock and cream. Add just enough to cover the vegetables – you can thin the soup further later with the additional stock if you like. Bring to the boil, then reduce the heat and simmer until all of the vegetables have softened completely.

3 Remove the pan from the heat and, using a hand-held electric blender, blitz the soup until smooth. Alternatively, use a food processor. Adjust the consistency with the addition of some more stock, if you like, then season to taste. Return the pan to the heat and reheat gently.

4 Serve immediately.

PEA AND MINT SOUP

A small portion of this soup is plenty, so it is delicious just as a taster at the start of a dinner party. Sometimes I add smoked bacon lardons or crisp Parma ham (prosciutto) to give the dish an extra element. The cheesy toasts can be prepared well in advance if needed.

SERVES 6

25g/1oz/¼ stick butter or sunflower oil, for cooking

1 large onion, peeled and chopped

1 medium potato, peeled and chopped

2 garlic cloves, peeled and chopped

450g/1lb/3 cups frozen peas

Salt and cracked black pepper

700ml/1¼ pints/3 cups chicken or vegetable stock (see pages 203–4)

125ml/4fl oz/½ cup pouring cream

3 tbsp chopped fresh mint

CHEESY TOASTS

1 ciabatta bread loaf or 1 medium bread roll

50g/2oz/¼ cup garlic butter

75g/3oz/¾ cup freshly grated cheese of choice

1 Melt the butter or heat a drizzle of oil in a large saucepan, add the onion, potato and garlic and sauté for a few minutes until lightly browned. Add the frozen peas and stir for a moment or two until they begin to defrost (they will begin to sizzle the moment they hit the pan). Add a pinch of salt and a grinding of black pepper at this stage.

2 Next pour in the stock and the cream and bring the mixture to a rapid boil. Reduce the heat and simmer for 12–15 minutes or until the peas have softened yet still retained their green colour.

3 Add the mint 1–2 minutes before you are ready to blitz the soup. Transfer the soup to a food processor and blitz in batches until smooth. Return the soup to a clean saucepan, taste and adjust the seasoning accordingly and reheat gently.

4 To make the cheesy toasts, preheat the grill or if using the oven preheat to 190°C (375°F) Gas mark 5.

5 Thinly slice the bread and butter lightly with the garlic butter then place on a baking tray and grill or bake in the oven for 4–5 minutes. Remove from the oven, sprinkle lightly with the grated cheese and return to the oven or place under the grill for a further moment until the cheese has melted. Store until required.

6 Serve the soup with the cheesy toasts.

CHICKEN AND CORN CHOWDER

Soup is always a great recipe for home entertaining, as it can be made in advance and just reheated as required. For dinner parties I like to serve just a small amount of this soup in little china cups, which makes it look more attractive and turns a basic bowl of soup into something a little bit special.

SERVES 8

2 large potatoes, peeled and chopped

3 celery sticks, sliced

2 carrots, peeled and diced

1 leek, trimmed and sliced

1 medium onion, peeled and diced

2 garlic cloves, peeled and crushed

50g/2oz/½ stick butter

3 large fresh thyme sprigs, plus extra to garnish

50g/2oz/⅓ cup plain (all-purpose) flour

About 900ml/1½ pints/3½ cups chicken stock (see page 203)

400g/14oz cooked chicken

200g/7oz/¾ cup tinned (canned) sweetcorn (corn)

250ml/9fl oz/1 cup pouring cream

Salt and freshly ground black pepper

1 Place the potatoes, celery, carrots, leek, onion and garlic in a large bowl.

2 Heat a large saucepan with the butter, toss in all the vegetables together with the thyme sprigs and cook gently over a low heat and without colouring for 8–10 minutes or until the smaller vegetables are beginning to soften. Sprinkle in the flour and stir until any liquid in the pan has dried up.

3 Next add the stock (about three-quarters of the stock would be enough at this time) and bring the mixture to a slow boil. Reduce the heat and simmer for a further 15–20 minutes or until all of the vegetables including the potatoes have softened down completely.

4 Shred the cooked chicken (I find that chicken legs left over after Sunday lunch are ideal for this). Remove the pan from the heat and add the shredded chicken to the soup together with the sweetcorn. Mix in the cream at this stage.

5 Return the pan to the heat and bring back to a very gentle boil. If you would like a thinner soup, now would be the best time to add any additional stock or cream to thin it down. Taste and adjust the seasoning accordingly.

6 Divide the soup among serving bowls or cups, garnish with a sprig of thyme if you like and serve.

TIP

I like to serve this soup as a nice chunky chowder-style soup, but alternatively, you can blitz it down to make a puréed soup.

OXTAIL SOUP

Oxtail soup has been around for ever. It is a gravy-like soup, which became popular in the UK in the eighteenth century and is now enjoying a renaissance.

SERVES 6–8

25g/1oz/¼ stick butter

150g/5oz turnip, diced

2 large carrots, peeled and diced

1 large onion, peeled and diced

2 celery sticks, diced

2 fresh thyme sprigs

50g/2oz/⅓ cup plain (all-purpose) flour

1 tsp tomato purée (tomato paste)

900g/2lb oxtail, jointed

1.25 litres/2 pints/5 cups beef stock (see page 202)

1 glass red wine

Chopped fresh parsley, to garnish

Crusty bread, to serve

1 Heat a large saucepan with the butter, add the diced vegetables together with the thyme sprigs and sauté for a few minutes until lightly browned.

2 Next add the flour and tomato purée and stir until all the vegetables are coated. Place the oxtail on top of the vegetables then pour in the stock and red wine and bring to the boil. Reduce the heat to very low and skim the scum off the surface with a slotted spoon. Continue to cook the soup over a very low heat for about 3 hours, adding a little additional stock if necessary.

3 Remove the oxtail from the soup and allow to cool, then shred all the meat from the tail.

4 Using a hand-held electric blender, blitz the vegetables and liquid into a thick soup, again adding some additional stock if you would like a soup of a different consistency. Alternatively, use a food processor. Add the shredded oxtail to the soup and gently reheat. Garnish with chopped parsley and serve immediately with crusty bread.

CRAB BISQUE

Crab is such a delightful starter (appetizer) ingredient. After extracting all the delicious crabmeat for other dishes (such as the Asian Crab Cakes on page 48), I love to use the shells to make this wonderful bisque.

SERVES 6–8

15g/½ oz/⅛ stick tbsp butter

1 onion, peeled and roughly chopped

2 carrots, peeled and roughly chopped

1 celery stick, roughly chopped

4 fresh thyme sprigs

2 bay leaves

3 fresh tarragon sprigs

4 crab shells, broken into pieces

¼ tsp cayenne pepper

1 tbsp tomato purée (tomato paste)

1 small glass white wine

25ml/1fl oz/⅛ cup brandy

1.25 litres/2 pints/5 cups hot fish stock (see page 205)

3 tbsp double (heavy) cream

Juice of ½ lemon

Salt and freshly ground black pepper

1 Melt the butter in a large frying pan until foaming, add the onion, carrots, celery and herbs and stir well. Fry for 2–3 minutes or until the vegetables have softened. Add the crab shell pieces, cayenne pepper and tomato purée and cook for a further 1–2 minutes.

2 Pour in the white wine and brandy and remove the pan from the heat. Set the mixture alight with a match, taking care to keep the flames away from your face, hands and other objects in the vicinity, and ensuring your extractor fan is turned off. Let the flames flare up then die down, and return the pan to the heat. Add the hot stock and bring to the boil. Reduce the heat and simmer for 30 minutes.

3 Remove the pan from the heat and remove and discard the crab shell pieces. Allow to cool slightly then transfer the mixture to a food processor and blitz to a purée.

4 Press the puréed mixture through a fine sieve (strainer) set over a clean pan. Add the cream and lemon juice to the pan, season to taste with salt and pepper and reheat gently before serving.

CHAPTER 2
STARTERS

Some people underestimate the value and importance of starters (appetizers). A good starter should excite and test all of the senses, setting the ball rolling for a most enjoyable meal.

In the restaurant, we find that the starters are where our guests are most daring with what they order and willing to experiment with something new. Often, they may even select two starters instead of a main course.

There are two occasions when you'll want to use this chapter. You may need a starter for a dinner party, but there are also many recipes here that are suitable as light lunch options. I have tried to give a variety of meat, fish and vegetarian ideas to help with your home entertaining needs. I also believe that a main prerequisite for a dinner party is that at least one of your courses can be prepared in advance, so many of the recipes in this section can be prepared ahead of time and enjoyed later, when you are ready for them.

VEGETARIAN SPRING ROLLS

These spring rolls are a great 'Get Out of Jail Free' card, in that you can turn to them when you need a kitchen shortcut. They can be quickly made up from fresh, or made ahead and kept in the freezer until needed. In this recipe I have used only vegetables, but of course you could add some duck, chicken, fish or beef into the mix as well. If you can't find spring roll pastry then use filo (phyllo) pastry instead but put two sheets together as it isn't as strong as spring roll pastry.

SERVES 8 (V)

Sunflower oil, for cooking

½ green chilli, diced

2 garlic cloves, peeled and diced

2.5cm/1in piece fresh root ginger (gingerroot), peeled and diced

2 celery sticks, sliced into 5cm/2in strips

1 leek (white part only), sliced into 5cm/2in strips

1 carrot, peeled and sliced into 5cm/2in strips

1 red onion, peeled and sliced into 5cm/2in strips

1½ (bell) peppers, mixed colours, sliced into 5cm/2in strips

50g/2oz cabbage, shredded into 5cm/2in strips

50g/2oz/½ cup beansprouts

Salt and freshly ground black pepper

2 tbsp sweet chilli sauce

8 sheets spring roll pastry

EGG WASH

1 egg

50ml/2fl oz/¼ cup milk

1 Heat a large wok then add a little oil. When the oil is hot, add the chilli, garlic and ginger and cook gently for 2–3 minutes. Add the vegetables and season lightly with salt and pepper and stir-fry for 3–4 minutes until the vegetables are beginning to soften. When the vegetables are fully cooked, add the chilli sauce. Transfer the mixture to a bowl and allow to cool completely.

2 For the egg wash, mix the egg and milk together and set aside.

3 Lay one sheet of the spring roll pastry on the work surface (counter) so that one of the corners points towards you. Brush around the edges with a little of the egg wash and then spoon about 1 tablespoon of the vegetable filling in a line near the top corner. Fold over to enclose then roll it towards you a little. Fold in the sides and continue to roll up into a nice cylindrical shape. Place the roll on a non-stick baking sheet and repeat with the remaining ingredients until you have eight spring rolls in total. Lightly brush with the remaining egg wash and chill for 30 minutes.

4 When ready to serve, pour enough oil into a deep-fat fryer or deep-sided saucepan to a depth of 6–7.5cm/2½–3in and heat to 180°C (350°F) or until a small piece of white bread turns golden

brown in about 30 seconds. Deep-fry the spring rolls for 3–4 minutes or until crisp on all sides and lightly golden. Remove with a slotted spoon and drain well on kitchen paper (paper towels).

5 To serve, use a sharp knife to cut off the very ends of each spring roll so that they will sit well on the plate, then cut each one in half on the diagonal. These are delicious served with some additional sweet chilli sauce.

SPICED CHICKPEA CAKES

_____

These spicy cakes are a delicious vegetarian starter and will definitely be a favourite with your guests.

SERVES 6 (V)

1 x 400g tin (can) chickpeas, rinsed and drained

Sunflower oil, for frying

½ red chilli, finely chopped

1 (bell) pepper, diced (½ green and ½ red)

2 garlic cloves, peeled and chopped

1 red onion, peeled and finely chopped

2.5cm/1in piece fresh root ginger (gingerroot), peeled and chopped

1 tbsp natural (plain) yoghurt

2 tsp curry powder

2 tbsp chopped fresh coriander (cilantro)

Plain (all-purpose) flour, for dusting

Large salad, to serve

1 Put the drained chickpeas into a food processor and blitz to a coarse purée.

2 Heat a little oil in a pan, add the chilli, peppers, garlic, onion and ginger and fry until soft. Remove the pan from the heat and allow to cool.

3 Transfer the chickpea purée to a large bowl, add the vegetable mixture and mix together until combined. Add the yoghurt, curry powder and coriander. Using floured hands, divide the mixture into 12 balls then shape into little patties.

4 Preheat the oven to 180°C (350°F), Gas mark 4.

5 Heat 1 tablespoon of oil in a large pan and fry the chickpea cakes, in batches, on both sides then bake in the oven for 10–12 minutes until piping hot. Serve immediately with a large salad.

POACHED PEARS
WITH CASHEL BLUE CHEESE

The flavour of blue cheese works wonderfully with poached pears. I chose to include this recipe in the starters chapter, but it could also be served as a dessert because it's almost a cross between a pudding and a cheeseboard.

SERVES 4 (V)

4 firm, ripe pears

1 small lemon, cut into quarters

1 small orange, cut into quarters

250g/9oz/1¼ cups caster (superfine) sugar

500ml/18fl oz/generous 2 cups red wine

350g/12oz Cashel Blue cheese

1 Peel the pears, leaving the stalks in place, and remove the cores. Stand them upright in a pan large enough to fit the pears comfortably and add the lemon, orange, sugar and wine. Add a little water if the pears are not completely covered in liquid then bring to a simmer. Cook for 40–45 minutes or until the pears are completely tender. Remove the pan from the heat and set aside to cool in the liquid for at least 2 hours or preferably overnight.

2 When ready to serve, drain the poaching liquid from the pears into a small pan and simmer over a low heat until reduced by half or until thickened and syrupy.

3 To serve, arrange the pears on four serving plates and, using a knife, cut into slices, leaving the stalks intact, then fan out the slices decoratively. Drizzle a little of the reduced syrup over each one – the remainder can be served in a small jug (pitcher) separately.

4 Slice the Cashel Blue cheese into thick wedges and arrange decoratively on the plates with the pears.

TIP

A soft goat's cheese also works very well with the pears.

ROASTED GARLIC RISOTTO

Many people panic at the idea of making risotto, but it is actually a very simple dish to create. The critical stage is at the addition of the stock – the best approach is to add just a little at a time and to continue tasting the rice until you are happy with its consistency.

SERVES 6–8

1 head of garlic, unpeeled

Salt and cracked black pepper

700ml/1¼ pints/3 cups chicken stock (see page 203)

25g/1oz/¼ stick butter

2 shallots, peeled and finely diced

½ tsp chopped fresh thyme

350g/12oz/generous 1½ cups Arborio (risotto) rice

½ glass dry white wine

100ml/3½fl oz/scant ½ cup pouring cream (optional)

75g/3oz/¾ cup freshly grated Parmesan cheese, plus extra to serve (optional)

1 Preheat the oven to 180°C (350°F), Gas mark 4.

2 Cut the garlic in half across, place in a small roasting tin and sprinkle with some salt. Roast the garlic for 35 minutes or until it has softened. Allow to cool and then squeeze all of the flesh out.

3 Bring the chicken stock to the boil in a saucepan.

4 Slowly melt the butter in a wide heavy-based saucepan over a low heat, add the diced shallots and thyme and cook very gently until the shallots have completely softened. Add the rice and stir well to make sure that it does not stick to the base of the pan, then cook over a low heat for 3–4 minutes, stirring constantly. This allows the rice to become glazed with the butter. Next, add the white wine and continue to stir until the wine is absorbed.

5 Add a ladleful of the boiling stock to the rice and stir. Continue to stir and add the stock little by little and never adding the next ladle until the previous one has been absorbed. It is important not to rush this process and to continue to add all of the liquid until the rice is plump and tender.

6 Season the risotto now with salt and pepper and stir in the roasted garlic purée. If you wish to have a nice rich and creamy risotto, add the cream and Parmesan cheese now. Adding just Parmesan will also make the risotto creamy. Serve immediately with additional Parmesan cheese, if you like.

TIP
It's important to keep the chicken stock hot at all times. If the stock is allowed to cool it will make the risotto stodgy.

BAKED EGGS
WITH SPINACH AND PARMESAN

What a lovely option for a tasty breakfast in bed! For a spicier version, try adding a little chorizo to the spinach. If you don't want to use spinach you could use thinly sliced leeks.

SERVES 4

A small knob of butter

110g/4oz/3 cups baby spinach leaves, washed and thoroughly dried

A pinch of freshly grated nutmeg

8 eggs

4 tbsp pouring cream

75g/3oz/¾ cup freshly grated Parmesan cheese

Cracked black pepper

Well-buttered toast, to serve

EQUIPMENT

Four small ramekins or ovenproof dishes

1 Preheat the oven to 190°C (375°F), Gas mark 5.

2 Begin by heating a frying pan with the butter and cooking the spinach over a high heat for about 1 minute or until the spinach has wilted. Once this has happened, sprinkle the spinach with the nutmeg – not too much, or it makes the dish very highly flavoured, which is undesirable.

3 Transfer the spinach to a fine sieve (strainer) and allow it to drain all the excess liquid. Push the spinach with the back of a spoon if that helps.

4 Divide the spinach among the four ramekins and then crack two eggs on top of each portion of spinach. Pour 1 tablespoon of cream over the eggs and then sprinkle the grated Parmesan over the top. Season with cracked black pepper.

5 Put the ramekins on a flat baking sheet and bake in the oven for about 15 minutes or until the eggs have just set. Serve immediately with slices of well-buttered toast.

DEEP-FRIED BRIE
WITH PLUM CHUTNEY

I love all types of cheese, but I love it even more when it's cooked. This is an old-fashioned style of recipe, but it is one of my favourites that I make quite regularly as a starter (appetizer) for Sunday lunch. The tartness of the plum chutney contrasts nicely with the soft creaminess of the cheese.

SERVES 4–6 (V)

450g/1lb Brie

50g/2oz/⅓ cup plain (all-purpose) flour

Salt and freshly ground black pepper

1 large egg beaten with about 100ml/3½fl oz/scant ½ cup milk

175g/6oz/3½ cups fresh white breadcrumbs

1 tbsp chopped fresh parsley

Vegetable or sunflower oil, for deep-frying

Salad leaves (salad greens), to serve

PLUM CHUTNEY

4 plums, stoned (pitted) and diced into rough chunks

1 large cooking apple, peeled, cored and diced

50g/2oz/⅓ cup sultanas (golden raisins)

2 tsp sunflower oil

50g/2oz/¼ cup (solidly packed) brown sugar

50ml/2fl oz/¼ cup red wine

50ml/2fl oz/¼ cup red wine vinegar

1 small cinnamon stick

1 Begin by making the plum chutney. Place the diced plums into a large saucepan with the diced apples, sultanas and the oil and cook gently until the pan is slightly heated. Next add the brown sugar and stir until it has dissolved and coated the fruit in a light caramel layer. Pour in the red wine and wine vinegar and bring to the boil. Pop in the cinnamon stick and allow the mixture to cook for at least 10 minutes over a medium heat or until all of the liquid is reduced. Transfer to a sterilised jar and store until required. This chutney will happily keep for 5–7 weeks.

2 To make the deep-fried Brie, cut the Brie cheese into large wedges.

3 Prepare three bowls, one with the flour with the addition of a little salt and pepper, a second with the beaten egg and milk and a third with the breadcrumbs and chopped parsley.

4 Put the cheese wedges into the seasoned flour and turn until coated, then shake off the flour. Transfer the cheese wedges to the egg and milk mixture, turn until coated then shake off the excess and place in the breadcrumbs and turn until coated. If you are nervous of the cheese melting too much in the deep-fat fryer, you could repeat the entire process again to give a second coating. Transfer the cheese to the fridge and allow to rest until you are ready to cook it.

5 Heat the oil for deep-frying in a deep-fat fryer or deep-sided saucepan to 180°C (350°F) or until a small piece of white bread turns golden brown in about 30 seconds. Carefully drop the cheese wedges into the hot oil and deep-fry for about 2 minutes or until the breadcrumbs have turned golden brown. Remove with a slotted spoon and drain on kitchen paper (paper towels). Serve immediately with a large spoonful of the plum chutney and some fresh salad leaves.

POTTED SHRIMP

The beauty of this starter (appetizer) is how few ingredients it needs and how quick it is to make. One of my personal favourites, Catherine and I often have this for supper, but I also like to make it for dinner parties as it's a stylish dish, perfect for formal occasions.

SERVES 6

110g/4oz/1 stick butter

450g/1lb raw langoustines (Norway lobster), peeled and de-veined

½ tsp cayenne pepper

Salt and freshly ground black pepper

6 small fresh thyme sprigs

TO SERVE

Brown bread

Lemon wedges

Green salad

EQUIPMENT

6 small pots or ramekins

1 Heat the butter in a large wide-based saucepan, add the langoustines together with the cayenne pepper and heat gently without boiling. Once the langoustines are gently cooked, season lightly with a little salt and pepper then divide the langoustines among the small pots or ramekins and press down gently.

2 Divide any of the remaining butter still in the pan among the pots or ramekins then put a small sprig of thyme on top of the butter and, using a spoon, press it down into the butter slightly. Grind some black pepper over the top.

3 Place the pots or ramekins in the fridge for a few hours until set. Serve the potted shrimp with some brown bread, lemon wedges and a large green salad.

ROASTED VEGETABLE SALAD

This salad is substantial enough to serve on its own, or can be served as part of a barbecue or buffet. You could also try adding some Parmesan shavings or chunks of feta or goat's cheese for an extra element. The salad will keep happily in the fridge for 3–4 days.

SERVES 6–8 (V)

2 aubergines (eggplants), chopped into large chunks or slices

3 red (bell) peppers, chopped into large chunks or slices

3 green (bell) peppers, chopped into large chunks or slices

2 courgettes (zucchini), chopped into large chunks or slices

I red onion, unpeeled and quartered

I garlic bulb, unpeeled and chopped

3 ripe plum tomatoes, chopped into large chunks

5 tbsp olive oil

Salt and freshly ground black pepper

A pinch of chopped fresh rosemary

A pinch of chopped fresh thyme

3 tbsp balsamic vinegar

I tbsp chopped fresh flat-leaf parsley

I Preheat the oven to 190°C (375°F), Gas mark 5.

2 Place all the vegetables in a large roasting tray and drizzle with about 2 tablespoons of olive oil then season lightly with a little salt and pepper. Add the chopped rosemary and thyme to the tray and roast in the oven for 20–25 minutes. Remove from the oven and allow to cool.

3 Once the roasted vegetables are cool, peel the onion and garlic and place them with the remaining vegetables in a large bowl with the rest of the olive oil, the balsamic vinegar and parsley. Season to taste and stir gently to combine. Either use immediately or chill, covered with clingfilm (plastic wrap), until ready to use. Just make sure to give it enough time to come back up to room temperature first. To serve, spoon the roasted vegetable salad on to serving plates.

TIP
Alternatively, cook the sliced vegetables on a hot barbecue (grill). Mix together the remaining olive oil, the vinegar and the parsley and pour over the roasted vegetables.

WARM SALAD OF GORGONZOLA CHEESE AND HONEY ROASTED PEACHES

The sweetness of the fruit in this salad works wonderfully alongside the delicious creamy flavour of the cheese. It's a beautifully simple recipe but one that looks and tastes gorgeous and your guests will be talking about it long after the meal has finished.

SERVES 4

25g/1oz/¼ stick butter

4 large peaches, halved or quartered and stoned (pitted)

150ml/5fl oz/⅔ cup runny honey

Juice of ½ lemon

2 fresh thyme sprigs

Mixed lettuce leaves (salad greens)

110g/4oz Gorgonzola cheese, crumbled

1 Melt the butter in a large frying pan until bubbling, add the peaches and mix them around until they are coated in the butter. Cook gently for 2 minutes until just beginning to soften. Add the honey to the pan together with the lemon juice and the thyme, then bring the mixture to the boil and cook for 1–2 minutes until the peaches are fully caramelised, which will happen because of the honey reduction. Remove the pan from the heat and allow the mixture to cool slightly for a moment or two.

2 Arrange the lettuce leaves in large bowls. Top with the crumbled Gorgonzola cheese and neatly arrange the roasted peaches on top. Drizzle with the thyme-infused honey left in the pan and serve.

ROASTED VEGETABLE COUSCOUS SALAD

Couscous itself can be quite bland, so it's important to add lots of different flavours, such as these roasted vegetables, to really bring it to life.

SERVES 6–8

1½ mixed (bell) peppers, such as red, green and yellow, chopped into bite-sized pieces

1 large red onion, peeled and chopped into bite-sized pieces

1 large courgette (zucchini), chopped into bite-sized pieces

1 small aubergine (eggplant), chopped into bite-sized pieces

12 cherry tomatoes, diced

25ml/1fl oz/⅛ cup olive oil

225g/8oz/1⅓ cups couscous

500ml/18fl oz/generous 2 cups chicken stock (see page 203)

Salt and freshly ground black pepper

Juice and finely grated zest of 1 lemon

4 tsp chopped fresh mint

4 tsp Basil Pesto (see page 208)

1 Preheat the oven to 190°C (375°F), Gas mark 5

2 Arrange the chopped vegetables on a baking tray, scatter the cherry tomatoes on top and drizzle with some of the olive oil. Roast in the oven for 15 minutes then allow to cool.

3 Place the couscous in a heatproof bowl. Bring the stock to the boil in a saucepan and pour over the couscous. Cover the bowl and set aside to rest for 10 minutes.

4 Use a fork to shake up the couscous then add the vegetables. Season well with salt and pepper, then mix in the lemon zest and juice, mint and remaining olive oil. Add the pesto and mix to bind it all together. Taste and adjust the seasoning accordingly, then either serve immediately or chill in the fridge until ready to serve.

CAESAR SALAD

Caesar salad must be the most popular salad in existence, judging by how frequently it gets ordered in restaurants. It is a very simple dish to make at home and is suitable as a starter (appetizer) or alternatively as a light lunch.

SERVES 4–6

4 slices of bread (slightly stale bread is best)

Sunflower oil, for cooking

175g/6oz/⅔ cup bacon lardons

1 large head cos (romaine) lettuce

75g/3oz/¾ cup freshly grated Parmesan cheese

CAESAR DRESSING

50g/2oz/½ cup freshly grated Parmesan cheese

3 egg yolks

3 garlic cloves, peeled

25g/1oz tinned (canned) anchovies

350ml/12fl oz/1½ cups olive or sunflower oil (sometimes a combination is nice)

Salt and freshly ground black pepper

1 Begin by making the Caesar dressing. Put the Parmesan cheese, egg yolks, garlic and anchovies into a food processor and blitz to a rough paste. Don't over-process or the eggs will over-thicken. It is possible to add the oil to the food processor, but the dressing may curdle and split, so I prefer to transfer the egg and anchovy paste to a large mixing bowl, then slowly pour in the oil and whisk thoroughly until the mixture has emulsified. Season to taste and store in the fridge until required. If the dressing is too thick whisk in a little milk or water to thin it down.

2 Meanwhile, cut the crusts off the bread then cut the bread into 1cm/½in cubes. Heat a large frying pan with a little oil. Add the cubes of bread to the hot pan and stir constantly until lightly browned. Remove with a slotted spoon and drain on kitchen paper (paper towels). Store until required (these can be stored for up to 1 week in an airtight container).

3 Clean out the pan and heat it, again with a little oil. Add the bacon lardons and allow them to brown up nicely. Cooking them on quite a high heat allows them to get nice and crispy. Remove with a slotted spoon and drain on kitchen paper.

4 To assemble the salad, tear the lettuce into a large mixing bowl. Add the bacon lardons and the croûtons then add a couple of tablespoons of the dressing to the salad and toss until coated. Transfer the salad to a large serving bowl and top with the grated Parmesan cheese.

VARIATION

Feel free to substitute the bacon for some poached or smoked chicken or salmon.

EGG MAYONNAISE

This recipe has really stood the test of time. It is most recognised these days as a sandwich filling, but I adore it and think it's good enough to be served as a starter (appetizer). It is best enjoyed simply with a slice of nice brown bread.

SERVES 6 (V)

6 fresh eggs

I small head iceberg lettuce, finely shredded

A pinch of paprika

Brown bread, to serve

MAYONNAISE

2 egg yolks

½ tsp dry mustard powder

I garlic clove, peeled and crushed

2 tsp white wine vinegar

250ml/9fl oz/I cup sunflower oil

Salt and freshly ground black pepper

POSSIBLE GARNISHES

Tomatoes

Cucumber

Finely diced (bell) peppers

Spring onions (scallions)

Red onions

Grated carrot

Beetroot (beet)

I To make the mayonnaise, place the egg yolks, mustard powder, crushed garlic and wine vinegar in a large mixing bowl and whisk well until combined, using either a hand whisk or an electric whisk. Very slowly begin to add the oil. For the first few drops beat it in very well between each addition then continue to pour in the oil and whisk well to allow the mixture to emulsify. If the mayonnaise is a little thick, you can whisk in 2 tablespoons of boiling water to correct the consistency. Season to taste with salt and pepper and store in a glass jar in the fridge for 3–4 days until required.

2 Meanwhile, place the eggs in a large saucepan of cold salted water, bring to the boil and boil for 6–8 minutes. Remove the eggs from the water with a slotted spoon and place in a large sieve (strainer). Leave them under cold running water for about 4–6 minutes until the eggs are completely cold. This will prevent a black or darkened rim forming around the cooked egg yolk. Once the eggs have cooled, peel and leave in the fridge until required.

3 Meanwhile, prepare the serving plate. I normally put a little finely shredded iceberg lettuce on the plate and then arrange two halves of one egg on top of the lettuce. Garnish the plate as desired with some of the suggested garnishes and place a large spoonful of the mayonnaise on top of the egg. Sprinkle with a little paprika and serve with slices of brown bread.

CURRIED VEGETABLE SAMOSAS

This is party food at its best. These samosas have a mild curried flavour but you can vary the flavour as much as you like. This recipe is for vegetarian samosas, but it can also be a great way to use up any leftover bits of meat, such as cooked chicken or duck; just shred and add in with the vegetables.

SERVES 6 (V)

sunflower oil

I red (bell) pepper, thinly sliced

I green (bell) pepper, thinly sliced

I medium onion, peeled and thinly sliced

3 garlic cloves, peeled and thinly sliced

75g/3oz cauliflower, broken into florets

75g/3oz/¾ cup beansprouts

75g/3oz/¾ cup mangetout (snow peas)

I tsp Thai green curry paste

½ tsp ground cumin

2 tbsp chilli jam

I packet of filo (phyllo) pastry, naturally thawed

About 110g/4oz/I stick butter, melted

Vegetable or sunflower oil, for deep-frying (optional)

Mango chutney or a dipping sauce, to serve

TIP
Spring roll pastry, available from Asian markets, tends to be more resilient than filo pastry, so use that if you prefer.

1 Heat a large wok with a little oil, and when hot, add all the vegetables and stir-fry for about 2–3 minutes until they are lightly glazed. Next add the curry paste and stir-fry until the vegetables are coated in the paste. Add the cumin and chilli jam and stir-fry for a few minutes until everything has combined with the flavours and heated through. Transfer the vegetables to a bowl and allow to cool.

2 Meanwhile, lay the filo pastry sheets on the work surface (counter) and cut the sheets into 18cm/7in squares. Brush each individual square with melted butter and stick about three squares directly on top of each other to make the samosas strong enough.

3 Place a spoonful of the vegetable mixture in the centre of one of the pastry squares then fold over and secure tightly into a triangular shape. You can use a little additional melted butter if required, which will act as a glue to secure the pastry in place. Repeat this process with the remaining pastry and vegetable mixture. Store in the fridge until ready to cook.

4 Preheat the oven to 190°C (375°F), Gas mark 5 or heat enough oil for deep-frying in a deep-fat fryer or deep-sided saucepan to 180°C (350°F) or until a small piece of white bread turns golden brown in about 30 seconds. If baking in the oven, brush the samosas with the remaining melted butter then place on a baking tray lined with parchment paper and bake for 5–6 minutes on each side. Alternatively, deep-fry in the hot oil for 45 seconds until golden brown. Remove with a slotted spoon and drain on kitchen paper.

5 Serve the samosas with mango chutney or a dipping sauce.

TIGER PRAWNS WITH A MANGO SALSA

I love how tiger prawns (jumbo shrimp) have such a delicate flavour but with a great meaty texture. Mango is the perfect accompaniment; the combination of the two makes for a delicious light summer starter (appetizer)!

SERVES 4

4 slices of crusty bread

1 tbsp olive or sunflower oil

16 tiger prawns (jumbo shrimp)

Juice of ½ lime

Cracked black pepper

MANGO SALSA

1 large firm mango

1 bunch of spring onions (scallions), trimmed and chopped

1 tbsp chopped fresh coriander (cilantro)

½ red chilli

50ml/2fl oz/¼ cup olive oil

Juice of ½ lime

Salt and freshly ground black pepper

1 Begin by preparing the mango salsa. Choose a mango that is not too soft. An over-ripe mango will make a very soggy salsa. Cut the mango into 5mm/¼in cubes and place in a small bowl with the chopped spring onions and coriander.

2 Finely dice the red chilli and add this to the salsa as well. Make sure the chilli is diced very finely, as large chunks of chilli are unpleasant. Next pour in the olive oil and the lime juice then season lightly. Store in the fridge until required.

3 Preheat the barbecue or a griddle pan (grill pan). Brush the slices of bread with a little oil and toast on the barbecue or the griddle pan until golden brown on both sides.

4 Place the tiger prawns in a large bowl then sprinkle with the lime juice and a little cracked black pepper. Place the prawns on the barbecue or griddle pan and cook for about 2 minutes on each side.

5 Remove the prawns from the barbecue or griddle pan and serve on top of a piece of toasted bread with a spoonful of the mango salsa.

ASIAN CRAB CAKES

I normally make these fancy fishcakes as a starter (appetizer), but they are also good as a main course (entrée). You can buy ready-prepared crabmeat, or use whole crabs and save the shells for the Crab Bisque on page 24.

SERVES 6–12

3 large potatoes, unpeeled

450g/1lb prepared crabmeat

2 tsp sunflower oil, plus extra 2 tbsp for frying

½ red chilli, finely chopped

2 garlic cloves, peeled and crushed

½ red onion, peeled and finely chopped

2.5cm/1in piece fresh root ginger (gingerroot), peeled and grated

1 large egg yolk

Sweet chilli jam, to serve

COATING

75g/3oz/½ cup plain (all-purpose) flour

Salt and freshly ground black pepper

2 large eggs mixed with 5 tbsp milk

200g/7oz/4 cups fresh white breadcrumbs

1 tbsp sesame seeds

1 tsp dried chilli flakes

1 Cook the potatoes in a large saucepan of boiling water for about 15–20 minutes or until tender. Drain and set aside until cool enough to handle, then peel them. Return the potatoes to the pan and mash. Allow to cool.

2 Pick through the crabmeat to make sure that there are no bones or traces of shell.

3 Heat the 2 teaspoons of oil in a frying pan, add the chilli, garlic, onion and ginger and fry until everything has softened, then remove from the heat and allow to cool.

4 Once the potatoes and chilli mixture are cold, mix the potatoes, crabmeat and chilli mixture together with the egg yolk. Using damp hands, divide the mixture into 6–12 balls and flatten slightly into round cakes.

5 For the coating, prepare three bowls, one with seasoned flour, a second with the beaten egg and milk and a third with fresh breadcrumbs mixed with sesame seeds and chilli flakes.

6 Put the crab cakes into the seasoned flour and roll until coated, then shake off the flour. Transfer the cakes to the egg and milk mixture and turn until coated then shake off the excess. Place the crab cakes in the breadcrumbs and roll until coated all over. Place the crab cakes on a plate.

7 Heat the 2 tablespoons of oil in a large pan and fry the crab cakes for 2–3 minutes on each side until piping hot. Alternatively, bake them in an oven preheated to 190°C (375°F), Gas mark 5, for 12–15 minutes or until piping hot. Serve immediately with sweet chilli jam.

SMOKED SALMON WITH PICKLED CUCUMBER AND CITRUS CREME FRAICHE

I'm a firm believer that smoked salmon should be served as plain and as simply as possible. So I love this combination of ingredients, because the light flavours of the cucumber and lemon don't overwhelm the fish.

SERVES 4

I large cucumber

150ml/5fl oz/⅔ cup rice wine vinegar

4 tsp caster (superfine) sugar

¼ tsp chopped fresh dill

Cracked black pepper

I shallot, peeled and very finely diced

CITRUS CREME FRAICHE

75g/3oz/⅓ cup crème fraîche

Finely grated zest of I lemon

Finely grated zest and juice of I lime

I tbsp chopped fresh parsley

Salt and freshly ground black pepper

TO SERVE

4 large slices of smoked salmon

Salad leaves (salad greens)

2 lemons, cut into wedges

1 To make the citrus crème fraîche, place the crème fraîche in a mixing bowl and whisk for a moment or two to soften it. Add the grated lemon zest, grated lime zest and juice, chopped parsley and seasoning and mix well to incorporate. Transfer to a clean bowl and store in the fridge until required.

2 To pickle the cucumber, using a vegetable peeler, slice the cucumber into very long thin strips, then with a very sharp knife, cut each strip into long ribbons and place in a bowl. Be careful not to add any of the seeds, as this can make the pickled cucumber very soggy.

3 Gently heat the rice wine vinegar and sugar together in a small saucepan. Do not bring the mixture to the boil but merely a gentle simmer. Add the chopped dill, some cracked black pepper and the finely diced shallot to the bowl with the cucumber and then pour the warmed vinegar and sugar mixture on top. Allow this mixture to cool and if possible allow it to infuse and develop in flavour for a number of days before using.

4 To serve, arrange a slice of salmon flat on a serving platter. Garnish with some mixed lettuce leaves and lemon wedges. Place a dollop of citrus crème fraîche on the platter with the salmon and arrange a small pile of pickled cucumber on the side.

SALMON SALADE NICOISE

This particular recipe is a variation on the classic Provençal favourite, as it uses salmon instead of tuna. I like to serve it with a well-chilled, high-acidity white wine, to complement the strong flavours of the dish, such as Bellet or Palette, which you can find in most good off-licences.

SERVES 4

4 portions of salmon, about 175g/6oz each

8 new potatoes, scraped or scrubbed

Salt and freshly ground black pepper

8 quails' eggs, at room temperature

110g/4oz/¾ cup extra-fine French beans (green beans), trimmed

4 Little Gem (Boston) lettuce hearts, quartered lengthways and separated

4 ripe plum tomatoes, roughly chopped

1 red onion, peeled and finely sliced

6 anchovy fillets, cut lengthways into thin strips

16 black olives in brine, pitted and drained

8 fresh basil leaves, torn

MARINADE

100ml/3½fl oz/scant ½ cup extra-virgin olive oil

3 tbsp aged red wine vinegar

2 tbsp chopped fresh flat-leaf parsley

2 tbsp snipped fresh chives

2 garlic cloves, peeled and finely chopped

1 To make the marinade, place all the ingredients in a bowl, add 1 teaspoon each of salt and pepper, and whisk to combine.

2 Place the salmon in a shallow non-metallic dish and pour over half of the marinade. Cover with clingfilm (plastic wrap) and chill for 1–2 hours to allow the flavours to penetrate the salmon, turning every 30 minutes or so.

3 Place the potatoes in a pan of boiling salted water, then cover, reduce the heat and simmer for 10–12 minutes or until just tender. Drain and leave to cool completely, then cut into quarters lengthways.

4 Place the quails' eggs in a small pan and just cover with boiling water then cook for 4 minutes. Drain and rinse under cold running water, then remove the shells and cut each egg in half. Plunge the French beans into a pan of boiling salted water and blanch for a minute or so, then drain and refresh under cold running water.

5 Heat a griddle pan (grill pan) for 5 minutes. Remove the salmon from the marinade, shaking off any excess and set any remaining marinade aside. Cook the salmon for 5–6 minutes on each side, depending on how thick it is. When cooked, the fish should feel quite firm to the touch.

6 Arrange the lettuce leaves on serving plates or one large platter and add the potatoes, French beans, tomatoes, onion and anchovies. Put the salmon on top and drizzle over the remaining marinade. Scatter over the quails' eggs, olives and torn basil leaves to serve.

PAN-ROASTED SCALLOPS WITH A BRANDY CREAM REDUCTION

Scallops are a fabulous starter (appetizer) and serving them with a small amount of this rich sauce turns them into a delightful special-occasion treat.

SERVES 4

1 leek, trimmed

1 carrot, peeled

12 large scallops, corals removed

Salt and cracked black pepper

Sunflower oil, for drizzling

25g/1oz/¼ stick butter

1½ tbsp brandy

200ml/7fl oz/generous ¾ cup pouring cream

4 tsp chopped fresh flat-leaf parsley, plus extra sprigs to garnish

SWEET POTATO CRISPS

250ml/9fl oz/1 cup sunflower oil

1 large sweet potato

Salt and freshly ground black pepper

1 Chop the leek and carrot into very thin strips and set aside.

2 To make the sweet potato crisps, heat the oil in a deep-fat fryer or a deep-sided saucepan to 180°C (350°F) or until a small piece of white bread turns golden brown in about 30 seconds.

3 Peel the sweet potato and, using a very sharp knife or a vegetable peeler, cut the sweet potato into thin strips. Deep-fry the potato strips for 2–3 minutes, then remove with a slotted spoon and drain on kitchen paper (paper towels). If using a saucepan to deep-fry the crisps, then carefully drop the sweet potato strips into the hot oil in batches. Season with a little salt and pepper and set aside until required.

4 Meanwhile, heat a large frying pan. Season the scallops with a little salt and cracked black pepper, drizzle with a little oil and sear quickly in the hot pan. Just as they are almost cooked, add the butter, which will give the scallops a nice glaze.

5 Remove the scallops from the pan and leave in a warm place or in a low oven for a few moments.

6 Meanwhile, keep the pan hot and quickly stir-fry the leek and carrot strips until they are just softened. Stir in the brandy and remove the pan from the heat. Set the mixture alight with a match, taking care to keep the flames away from your face, hands and other objects in the vicinity, and ensuring your

extractor fan is turned off. Let the flames flare up then die down, and return the pan to the heat. Next add the cream and gently bring to the boil. Season to taste and then mix in the chopped parsley.

7 Spoon a little of the brandy and vegetable reduction onto a plate and top with three glazed scallops. Garnish with a sprig of flat-leaf parsley and the sweet potato crisps.

SMOKED SALMON AND LEMON PASTA

This dish is quick and easy to make but the ingredients are sophisticated and it looks most attractive when served up. It's bound to be a big hit with your family and friends.

SERVES 6 AS A STARTER, 4 AS MAIN COURSE

350g/12oz farfalle pasta

200ml/7fl oz/generous ¾ cup pouring cream

75g/3oz/⅓ cup cream cheese

Juice and finely grated zest of 1 lemon

½ glass white wine

50g/2oz/½ cup freshly grated Parmesan cheese, plus extra for sprinkling

175g/6oz smoked salmon, chopped into long strips

2 tbsp chopped fresh flat-leaf parsley

Salt and freshly ground black pepper

White Yeast Bread, to serve (see page 211)

1 Bring a large saucepan of water to the boil, add the pasta and cook according to the packet instructions.

2 Meanwhile, in another large saucepan, bring the cream, cream cheese and lemon juice and zest to the boil. Add the white wine and grated Parmesan and cook until heated through. Allow the sauce to cook for at least 10 minutes over a low heat, stirring occasionally, during which time it will thicken by process of reduction and also with the addition of the cheese. Season to taste with salt and pepper.

3 Drain the pasta, add to the hot sauce and mix until combined. Add the smoked salmon strips and the chopped parsley and mix well.

4 Transfer to a large serving dish, sprinkle over some additional Parmesan cheese and serve, allowing people to help themselves, with chunks of fresh white yeast bread.

BAKED SADDLE OF RABBIT
WITH PARSNIP PUREE

Rabbit is a very popular inclusion on our restaurant menu at Dunbrody House. Get your butcher to prepare the saddle for you. I find it is best to take it off the bone and to split it like a book, as this makes it easy to stuff.

SERVES 4

4 saddles of rabbit, about 200g/7oz each

110g/4oz coarse black pudding (blood sausage)

50ml/2fl oz/¼ cup pouring cream

½ tsp chopped fresh thyme

Salt and freshly ground black pepper

PARSNIP PUREE

2 parsnips, peeled and cut into chunks

1 tsp chopped fresh thyme

500ml/18fl oz/generous 2 cups milk

2 tbsp pouring cream (if required)

1 Preheat the oven to 190°C (375°F), Gas mark 5.

2 Remove the skin from the black pudding and put into a food processor with the cream and chopped thyme. Season lightly with a little salt and pepper and process until puréed.

3 Spoon the black pudding purée into a disposable piping bag (pastry bag) and pipe a line down the middle of each saddle of rabbit then fold the fillet over the black pudding purée to enclose and roll into a cylindrical shape.

4 Heat a medium frying pan and, when hot, add the rabbit and cook for 2–3 minutes until sealed on all sides. Place the rabbit on a baking sheet and cook in the oven for 10–12 minutes. Remove the rabbit from the oven and allow to rest while you make the parsnip purée.

5 To make the parsnip purée, place the parsnips in a large saucepan with the chopped thyme. Cover with the milk and bring to the boil, then reduce the heat and simmer for 15 minutes or until the parsnips are very soft.

6 Strain the parsnips through a sieve (strainer), keeping a little of the milk – about 2 tablespoons – to purée the parsnips.

7 Transfer the parsnips and reserved milk to a food processor and process until puréed then season. If you are not using the parsnip purée immediately, transfer it to a clean bowl and cover. Reheat the purée gently in a pan with the cream until hot. Serve as required.

CHICKEN LIVER PATE

This is a very simple recipe, but the result is a beautifully indulgent and extravagant dish, which is a favourite of many people.

SERVES 8–10

135g/5oz/1¼ stick butter softened

2 tsp sunflower oil

110g/4oz/scant ½ cup smoked bacon lardons

1 onion, peeeled and chopped

2 garlic cloves, peeled and crushed

450g/1lb chicken livers

3 bay leaves

75ml/3fl oz/⅓ cup brandy

Salt and freshly ground black pepper

About 110ml/4fl oz/½ cup clarified butter (see page 193)

EQUIPMENT

8–10 small ramekins

1 Heat 25g/1oz/¼ stick of the butter with the oil in a frying pan. Add the bacon, onion and garlic and cook over a low heat until the onions have softened. Add the chicken livers to the pan with the bay leaves then increase the heat and cook for 3–4 minutes until the livers are nicely browned on the outside but still pink and soft in the centre.

2 Add the brandy and simmer for a further 3 minutes. Remove and discard the bay leaves then transfer the mixture to a food processor and process until puréed. Gradually add the rest of the butter when the mixture is almost puréed. Season to taste with salt and pepper.

3 Spoon the mixture into the ramekins and cover with a small layer of clarified butter. Allow to rest in the fridge for at least 3 hours or preferably overnight. Use as required.

STICKY CHICKEN WINGS

Perfect party food! Chicken wings always go down well with a crowd and are simple to prepare in large quantities. The glaze of soy sauce, honey, chilli and ginger also works well as a marinade for salmon, pork or chicken breasts.

SERVES 6–8

2 tbsp runny honey

100ml/3½fl oz/scant ½ cup soy sauce

½ red chilli, finely chopped

2.5cm/1in piece fresh root ginger (gingerroot), peeled and freshly grated

18–24 chicken wings

100ml/3½fl oz/scant ½ cup chicken stock (see page 203), optional

Sesame seeds, for sprinkling

Boiled basmati rice, to serve

1 Place the honey, soy sauce, chilli and grated ginger in a large bowl and mix together. Add the chicken wings and mix thoroughly until all of the wings are coated with the sticky glazed mixture. If time allows, leave the wings to marinate overnight, but if not, a couple of hours will suffice.

2 Preheat the oven to 180°C (350°F), Gas mark 4.

3 Remove the chicken wings from the marinade, reserving the marinade, and arrange the chicken wings on a roasting tray. Cover with foil and bake for 20–25 minutes until the wings are almost fully cooked.

4 Meanwhile, heat the reserved marinade in a small saucepan and bring to a rapid boil for a moment or two – be careful at this stage, as the honey may have a tendency to burn. Sometimes, if I feel it is reducing too quickly, I will add some stock just to add extra liquid content to the marinade.

5 After the marinade has come to the boil, pour it over the chicken wings and mix to make sure that they are all coated with the marinade.

6 Increase the oven temperature to 200°C (400°F), Gas mark 6 and return the chicken wings with the marinade, uncovered, to the oven. Cook for a further 15–20 minutes at this stage, taking them out of the oven every so often to give them a little shake to prevent them from sticking to the tray but also ensuring that each of the wings is covered with the sticky glaze.

7 Serve the chicken wings sprinkled with sesame seeds and accompanied with plain boiled basmati rice – and a finger bowl!

LEMON TAGLIATELLE
WITH PANCETTA AND FRESH PEAS

This pasta is quick and easy to prepare and the lovely combination of colours just adds further to its appeal. You can vary the flavours by adding some cooked chicken or smoked salmon instead of the pancetta, or alternatively you can bulk up the dish with vegetables for a tasty vegetarian option.

SERVES 6

Butter, for frying

2 garlic cloves, peeled and diced

I shallot, peeled and finely diced

100ml/3½fl oz/scant ½ cup white wine

175ml/6fl oz/¾ cup pouring cream

Salt and freshly ground black pepper

Finely grated zest of I lemon

50g/2oz/½ cup freshly grated Parmesan cheese, plus extra to serve

75g/3oz/½ cup peas (fresh or frozen)

350g/12oz tagliatelle

6 very thin slices of pancetta

I Begin by heating a large pan with a little butter and very gently fry the garlic and shallot for 4–5 minutes until they are completely softened. Next pour in the white wine and the cream and allow this mixture to come to a rapid boil. Reduce the heat slightly and season the sauce with a little salt, grated lemon zest and lots of black pepper. Add the grated Parmesan, which will begin to thicken and flavour the sauce slightly. Add the peas at this stage and allow them to cook in the sauce.

2 Meanwhile, bring a large saucepan of water to the boil, add the tagliatelle and cook according to the packet instructions. Drain the pasta and mix the tagliatelle into the sauce. Tear some pieces of pancetta into the sauce and mix well.

3 Taste and adjust the seasoning accordingly and serve the pasta with some extra grated Parmesan.

AFRICAN BEEF SALAD
WITH BILTONG

Biltong is a kind of cured meat that originated in South Africa. It is typically made either from raw fillets of meat cut into strips along the grain of the muscle, or from flat pieces sliced across the grain. It is similar to beef jerky in that they are both spiced, dried meats, but they differ in their ingredients, production process and, ultimately, taste.

SERVES 6–8

2 slices of beef fillet (tenderloin), about 200g/7oz each

6–8 red (ruby) chard leaves

200g/7oz mixed lettuce

1 green (bell) pepper, thinly sliced

1 onion, peeled and diced

2 garlic cloves, peeled and diced

10–12 cherry tomatoes

1 tbsp biltong

MARINADE

1 tsp turmeric

2 cardamom pods

100ml/3½fl oz/scant ½ cup sunflower oil

Cracked black pepper

2 tsp runny honey

DRESSING

1 garlic clove, peeled and finely diced

Salt and freshly ground black pepper

2 tsp runny honey

Juice of ½ lemon

6 tsp olive oil

1 Begin by making the dressing. Place the garlic in a mixing bowl, season to taste with salt and pepper, then add the honey and lemon juice and mix thoroughly. Slowly pour in the oil and mix thoroughly until combined. Set aside.

2 Place all the ingredients for the marinade in a shallow non-metallic dish and mix together. Add the beef and turn a few times until coated in the marinade. Cover and allow to marinate for about 1 hour, turning occasionally, in a cool place or fridge.

3 Preheat the barbecue (grill). Remove the beef from the marinade and discard the marinade. Cook the beef either on a grill pan or on the hot bars of the barbecue to your liking – 2 minutes on either side for rare, 4 minutes on either side for medium and 5 minutes on either side for well done.

4 Meanwhile, mix the chard, lettuce, pepper, onion and garlic together in a large serving bowl. Add the cherry tomatoes and coat with the dressing. Thinly slice the beef and place it on top of the salad then sprinkle the biltong on top and serve.

CHICKEN AND PARMA HAM TERRINE WITH PISTACHIO NUTS

A terrine is so impressive to slice up at the table, and is also a great item to make for a summer picnic as it's quite transportable. The flavours in this terrine work particularly well together, and the nuts add a pleasant crunch.

SERVES 8

8 slices of Parma ham (prosciutto)

300g/11oz/1⅓ cups minced (ground) pork

50g/2oz/⅓ cup prunes, finely diced

50g/2oz/⅓ cup pistachio nuts

2 garlic cloves, peeled and finely diced

2 fresh thyme sprigs, chopped

½ tsp wholegrain mustard

Salt and freshly ground black pepper

2 tsp dried cranberries (optional)

2 skinless chicken breasts, sliced into long strips

200g/7oz chicken livers, roughly diced

6 asparagus spears

1 carrot, peeled and cut into long thin strips

TO SERVE

Green salad

Spiced tomato chutney or sweet chilli jam

EQUIPMENT

A 900g/2lb loaf tin (pan) or terrine mould

1 Preheat the oven to 150°C (300°F), Gas mark 2.

2 Line the loaf tin with the Parma ham, leaving an overhang around the edge to encase later on. Put the minced pork into a large bowl and then add the prunes, pistachios, garlic, thyme and mustard. Season with a little salt and pepper (not too much salt). If you are using the dried cranberries, add these now. If you are concerned about the seasoning in this dish, then mould a small portion of the mixture into a burger and fry it in a little oil for about 4 minutes on each side just to have a taste.

3 Divide the mixture into three portions. Place one-third of the mixture in the tin and top with some strips of chicken, some chicken livers, three asparagus spears and some carrot strips. Put another third of the minced pork mixture on top, then the chicken strips, chicken livers, asparagus spears and remaining carrot and top with the remaining minced pork mixture. Fold over the Parma ham and cover with a layer of foil.

4 Place the terrine into a bain-marie (a roasting tray half-filled with cold water) and bake in the oven for 1¼–1½ hours.

5 When the terrine is cooked, allow to cool, preferably overnight. When ready to serve, turn it out onto a serving plate, slice into thin slices and serve with a green salad and a little spiced tomato chutney or sweet chilli jam.

BARBECUED PORK WITH POTATO SALAD

––––––––

This recipe uses pork belly, which is an inexpensive cut of meat that at first glance can look rather fatty, but the majority of the fat gets cooked off when sealing the pork in the pan. It is best served quite simply, although the apple juice in the recipe imparts a wonderful succulence to the finished dish so is definitely worth including.

SERVES 4

1.5kg/3lb 5oz pork belly, rind removed

Salt and freshly ground black pepper

150ml/5fl oz/⅔ cup good-quality dry (hard) cider

300ml/10fl oz/1¼ cups chicken stock (see page 203)

1 star anise

5 fennel seeds, lightly crushed

1 onion, peeled and sliced

4 garlic cloves, peeled and sliced

4 fresh thyme sprigs

2 tbsp runny honey

2 tbsp dark soy sauce

About 300ml/10fl oz/1¼ cups freshly pressed apple juice

Beetroot relish (see tip overleaf), to serve (optional)

Ingredients continued ⟶

1 Preheat the oven to 180°C (350°F), Gas mark 4.

2 To prepare the pork, heat a large cast-iron frying pan. Season the pork belly with salt and pepper then add to the pan, fat side down and quickly sear on all sides to seal. Remove from the heat and allow to rest for about 5 minutes.

3 Pour the cider into a large jug (pitcher) with the chicken stock. Add the star anise and fennel seeds then season lightly with salt and set aside.

4 Place the onion in a roasting tin with the garlic and thyme, tossing to coat. Place the pork belly on top and pour around the cider mixture. Season to taste and cover with foil. Braise in the oven for 2½–3 hours until the pork is tender and completely soft. When the pork belly is cooked, transfer to a warm plate and allow to rest for at least 20 minutes.

5 To make the potato salad, cut the potatoes into 2.5cm/1in chunks. Place in a saucepan of salted water and bring to the boil. Cook for 12–15 minutes or until tender. This will depend on your potatoes, so keep an eye on them.

6 Meanwhile, whisk the white wine vinegar and olive oil together in a small bowl, and season to taste. Drain the potatoes well, transfer to a serving bowl and gently stir in the dressing. Allow to cool completely.

Continued ⟶

POTATO SALAD

900g/2lb small, waxy new
potatoes, scraped or
scrubbed

2 tsp white wine vinegar

2 tbsp light olive oil

Salt and freshly ground
black pepper

3 heaped tbsp mayonnaise

1 heaped tbsp crème fraîche

1 bunch of spring onions
(scallions), trimmed and
thinly sliced

2 tbsp chopped fresh dill

2 tbsp chopped fresh flat-
leaf parsley

7 When ready to finish cooking the pork, light the barbecue. Mix the honey and soy sauce together, then brush all over the rested pork belly. When the charcoal is ash-white, carefully put a shallow foil tray in the centre of the coals and pour in enough of the apple juice to come two-thirds of the way up.

8 Place the pork on a grill rack and set directly over the tray with the apple juice. Cook for 10–15 minutes on each side until the pork belly is nicely caramelised and sizzling, basting occasionally with the remaining soy sauce mixture. Top up the apple juice as necessary.

9 To finish the potato salad, stir the mayonnaise and crème fraîche together in a small bowl and stir into the potatoes with the spring onions, dill and parsley then season to taste. Carve the barbecued pork into slices and arrange on plates with the potato salad. Add a dollop of beetroot relish, if desired.

TIP

To make your own beetroot relish, finely chop four cooked baby beetroots – drained from a jar is fine – and place in a bowl. Stir in a finely chopped shallot and a light sprinkling of chopped fresh dill. Season to taste, then add a pinch of sugar and stir well to combine. Use as required.

MINI CHICKEN AND BLACK PUDDING PIES

These pies make quite a substantial starter (appetizer), so you might prefer them as a supper option. Try to use a coarse black pudding (blood sausage), as the interesting texture adds to the success of this the dish.

SERVES 6

Melted butter or sunflower oil, for brushing

I packet of puff pastry, naturally thawed

Plain (all-purpose) flour, for dusting

3 skinless chicken breasts, diced

200g/7oz black pudding (blood sausage)

175g/6oz/¾ cup cream cheese

25g/Ioz/½ cup fresh white breadcrumbs

I tbsp chopped fresh mixed herbs, such as parsley, thyme and rosemary

Green salad with mustard seed dressing, to serve

EGG WASH

I egg

50ml/2fl oz/¼ cup milk

EQUIPMENT

12-hole deep muffin tray

large biscuit (cookie) cutter or circular template

I Preheat the oven to 180°C (350°F), Gas mark 4. Brush six cups of the muffin tray lightly with melted butter or oil.

2 Roll out the puff pastry on a lightly floured work surface (counter) and use a large biscuit (cookie) cutter or some suitable-sized implement to cut out six discs. Line the inside of each of the prepared cups in the muffin tray with a pastry disc. Try to push the pastry over the top of the actual cup to allow for covering the pies later on.

3 Meanwhile, place the diced chicken in a large bowl with the black pudding and cream cheese. Add the breadcrumbs and chopped herbs and mix together well.

4 For the egg wash, mix the egg and milk together and set aside.

5 Divide the chicken mixture among the pastry-lined cups and then fold the little overhang you have at the top back in over the filling to form a lip. Brush the surface of this pastry lip with a little of the egg wash. This will act as a glue to stick the top on.

6 With the leftover pastry, cut out six more discs and stick one onto the top of each pie. Brush the top of the pies with the remaining egg wash, and with a sharp knife, make one or two incisions in the top of each pie.

7 Bake in the oven for about 30–35 minutes or until the pastry is golden brown and the chicken is fully cooked through to the centre. Serve with a green salad with some mustard seed dressing.

HAM HOCK
AND PARSLEY TERRINE

A terrine is ideal either as a fancy starter (appetizer) or as a nice picnic option. It does take a little bit of work to prepare, but the delicious and attractive final product is well worth the effort.

SERVES 6–8

1 ham hock, about 2kg/4lb 6oz (just under 900g/2lb when shredded off the bone)

2 onions, peeled and halved

3 celery sticks, trimmed and diced

2 carrots, peeled and diced

1 bay leaf

2 fresh thyme sprigs

6–8 cloves

8 black peppercorns

3 large fresh curly parsley sprigs (enough to make 2 tbsp when chopped)

2 shallots, peeled and diced

4 gherkins, diced

1 tsp Dijon mustard

1 tsp capers

Salt and cracked black pepper

3 gelatine leaves

EQUIPMENT

A 900g/2lb terrine mould or loaf tin (pan)

1 Soak the ham hock in cold water for 1 hour then put it in a large saucepan with all of the vegetables, bay leaf, thyme sprigs and spices. Bring to the boil, then reduce the heat and simmer for 2 hours or until the ham hock is nicely cooked and a skewer inserted into the ham meets with no resistance. Remove the ham from the pan and allow to cool. Strain the stock through a sieve into a pan and cook to reduce the liquid by about one-third then remove the pan from the heat.

2 Blanch the parsley sprigs in a saucepan of hot water for 20–30 seconds then plunge the parsley into a bowl of ice-cold water to refresh. Squeeze the parsley to get rid of all excess water and then chop it roughly.

3 Shred or chop the cooled meat into small pieces, keeping a small amount of the fat, then put the meat and fat into a large mixing bowl with the diced shallot, gherkins, Dijon mustard, capers and the parsley. Season with some cracked black pepper (be careful if you are adding salt) and mix well.

4 Line the terrine mould with clingfilm (plastic wrap) and press the meat mixture into the mould.

5 Meanwhile, gently heat 300ml/10fl oz/1¼ cups of the reduced stock.

6 Soak the gelatine in a bowl of cold water for 10 minutes then drain the liquid off using a fine sieve (strainer). Whisk the now softened gelatine into the stock and carefully pour this over the pressed meat. Chill overnight and then serve with a small salad.

CHAPTER 3

MAIN COURSES

The kind of dinners I love best are simple and hearty ones, so many of the recipes in this chapter are for straightforward, good old-fashioned comfort food. When I was a child, Mum would often make slow-cooked casseroles or have joints of meat cooking for hours on end in the oven and the results would be a gastronomic delight. Thanks to her, this is the style of cooking I tend to favour, both in my career and at home.

I have included many of my favourite meals that I have cooked and collected over the years, suitable for dining indoors or al fresco. There are also some more unusual recipes, which again came to me from my mother – she lived abroad for a number of years and her travels introduced her to some wonderful regional food, such as the African dish Bobotie.

GINGER SPICED VEGETABLE PIE

I get so many requests from vegetarians looking for interesting recipes. Sadly, many restaurants treat their vegetarian options as an afterthought but I think this recipe is good enough to tempt plenty of carnivores too.

SERVES 6 (V)

Sunflower oil, for cooking

3 garlic cloves, peeled and diced

2.5cm/1in piece fresh root ginger (gingerroot), peeled and diced

½ red chilli, finely diced

1 red, 1 yellow and 1 green (bell) pepper, thinly sliced

1 carrot, peeled and thinly sliced

½ courgette (zucchini), thinly sliced

75g/3oz/¾ cup mixed mushrooms, thinly sliced

1 red onion, thinly sliced

75g/3oz/¾ cup mangetout (snow peas)

3 tbsp sweet chilli relish, plus extra to serve

1 packet of puff pastry, naturally thawed

Plain (all-purpose) flour, for dusting

Large salad, to serve

EGG WASH

1 egg

2 tbsp milk

EQUIPMENT

20cm/8in loose-bottomed flan ring or tin (tart pan)

1 Heat a large wok with a little oil. Add the garlic, ginger and chilli and cook over a low heat to allow the oil to become infused with their flavour. Next add the vegetables, increase the heat to high and cook for 3–4 minutes until they are all nicely browned. Add the sweet chilli relish, immediately turn off the heat and transfer the vegetable stir-fry to a bowl to cool.

2 Meanwhile, roll out some of the puff pastry on a lightly floured work surface (counter) and use to line the flan ring. Roll out another piece for the top and, using a lattice cutter, score this pastry. If you do not have a lattice cutter, you can just cut the pastry into long thin strips and arrange them in a crisscross pattern at a later stage.

3 Once the vegetables have cooled, pour them into the middle of the lined pie case then roll or arrange the lattice over the top of the vegetables and press down lightly.

4 Preheat the oven to 190°C (375°F), Gas mark 5.

5 For the egg wash, beat the egg and milk together in a small bowl.

6 Brush the egg wash over the top of the pastry and bake in the oven for about 20 minutes until the pastry is well-risen and golden brown. Serve with a large salad and additional sweet chilli relish.

ASIAN VEGETABLE STIR-FRY

Climb aboard the Orient Express! A quick, simple and economical dish, but one that is always popular.

SERVES 8 (V)

1 tsp sunflower oil

2 garlic cloves, peeled and crushed

1 green chilli, very finely diced

1 carrot, peeled and thinly sliced

1 leek, trimmed and thinly sliced

2 celery sticks, thinly sliced

1½ mixed (bell) peppers, such as green, red and yellow, thinly sliced

1 red onion, peeled and thinly sliced

110g/4oz/generous 1 cup mangetout (snow peas)

100ml/3½fl oz/scant ½ cup vegetable stock (see page 204) or water

1½ tbsp medium sherry

1 tbsp runny honey

100ml/3½fl oz/scant ½ cup soy sauce

4 portions of egg noodles, blanched and refreshed (see tip)

Toasted sesame seeds, to garnish

1 Heat a large wok with the oil, add the garlic and chilli and fry over a high heat for 2–3 minutes until almost crispy. Add the vegetables and quickly fry them using a little stock or water if the mixture gets too dry. Try not to add any more oil – use the stock instead, else the stir-fry will be too oily. When everything is almost cooked, add the sherry, honey and soy sauce together with the noodles and heat thoroughly. Add more stock if required so it isn't too dry.

2 Serve immediately, garnished with toasted sesame seeds.

TIP
To blanch the noodles, cook in boiling salted water according to the packet instructions and then immerse in cold running water until sufficiently cold and the cooking process has been halted.

VEGETARIAN PASTA BAKE

A simple recipe for a quick and easy vegetarian main course (entrée) that will be popular with adults and kids alike. You can use any vegetables with this recipe, so just play around with what you have.

SERVES 6 (V)

350g/12oz penne pasta

Salt and freshly ground black pepper

Sunflower oil or butter, for cooking

2 garlic cloves, peeled and chopped into small pieces

1 red onion, peeled and thinly sliced

1½ mixed (bell) peppers, such as red, green and yellow, thinly sliced

½ head broccoli, broken into florets

6 mushrooms, thinly sliced

2 x 400g tins (cans) chopped tomatoes

50ml/2fl oz/¼ cup pouring cream

2 tsp chopped fresh mixed herbs, such as parsley, sage, rosemary and thyme

TOPPING

1 tbsp chopped fresh parsley

110g/4oz/generous 2 cups fresh white breadcrumbs

50g/2oz/½ cup grated vegetarian cheese, such as Cheddar, Gruyère, mozzarella

TO SERVE

Green salad

Garlic Bread (see page 100)

1 Cook the penne in a large pan of boiling salted water according to the packet instructions then drain.

2 Preheat the oven to 180°C (350°F), Gas mark 4.

3 Meanwhile, heat a large saucepan with a little oil or butter, add the garlic and cook slowly over a low heat for 4–5 minutes until soft. Next add the onion, peppers and broccoli together with the sliced mushrooms. Cook the vegetables for about 5 minutes or until they are softened. Next add the chopped tomatoes. (I normally wash out the can with a little extra water and add this to the dish just to make sure that you get all of the goodness of the tomatoes into the dish. Also it will make a delicious sauce.) Add the cream and bring the mixture to the boil. Add the mixed herbs and cooked pasta and adjust the seasoning accordingly. Pour the mixture into a large casserole dish.

4 To make the topping, mix all the ingredients together in a bowl and spread over the top of the pasta. Bake in the oven for 15–20 minutes until bubbling.

5 Serve with a green salad and garlic bread.

GARDEN CHERRY TOMATOES AND OLIVE LINGUINE

This is a very simple recipe for a pasta dish that is delicious hot, but equally tasty when served cold as a salad.

SERVES 6

400g/14oz fresh linguine

Olive oil, for cooking

Sea salt and cracked black pepper

1 medium onion, peeled and finely sliced

2 garlic cloves, peeled and finely chopped

110g/4oz cherry tomatoes, cut in half

110g/4oz/⅔ cup black olives, stoned (pitted)

100ml/3½fl oz/scant ½ cup dry white wine

2 tbsp roughly chopped fresh parsley

110g/4oz Parmesan cheese shavings, to garnish

Garlic Bread (see page 100), to serve

1 To cook the pasta, bring a large saucepan of water to the boil with a dash of olive oil and a pinch of salt over a high heat. Add the linguine and cook for 7 minutes, then drain.

2 Heat a large frying pan over a high heat then add a dash of olive oil. Add the onion and garlic and cook for 4 minutes until golden brown. Add the cherry tomatoes and olives then add the white wine and chopped parsley and season to taste with salt and black pepper. Remove the pan from the heat, add the linguine and toss until everything is combined.

3 Divide the pasta among pasta bowls and garnish with Parmesan shavings. Serve with large chunks of garlic bread.

WILD MUSHROOM, SPINACH AND BLUE CHEESE TART

A savoury tart or quiche is a great option to have in your repertoire for summer picnics and informal entertaining.

SERVES 8–10

SHORTCRUST PASTRY (PIE DOUGH)

300g/11oz/2 cups plain (all-purpose) flour, plus extra for dusting

A pinch of salt

150g/5oz/1¼ sticks hard butter, cut into pieces

2 tsp fennel seeds (optional)

FILLING

2 tsp sunflower oil

150g/5oz/1¼ cups mixed wild mushrooms

150g/5oz/4 cups baby spinach leaves

110g/4oz blue cheese

4 large eggs

250ml/9fl oz/1 cup milk

50ml/2fl oz/¼ cup pouring cream

1 tbsp chopped fresh parsley

Salt and freshly ground black pepper

TO SERVE

Large salad

EQUIPMENT

23cm/9in fluted flan dish (tart pan)

1 To make shortcrust pastry, sift the flour into a large mixing bowl and add the salt. Add the butter and, using your fingertips, rub the butter into the flour until the mixture resembles very fine breadcrumbs. Add the fennel seeds, if using, then gradually mix in enough ice cold water (about 4 teaspoons) until the mixture comes together into a ball. Knead the dough gently until smooth then cover with clingfilm (plastic wrap) and rest in the fridge for 1 hour.

2 Preheat the oven to 180°C (350°F), Gas mark 4.

3 Roll out the pastry on a lightly floured work surface (counter) and use to line a 23cm/9in fluted flan dish (tart pan). Blind bake (see tip on page 186) in the oven. Allow to cool.

4 For the filling, heat the oil in a large heavy-based pan and quickly fry the mushrooms for 4–5 minutes until cooked through, then add the spinach and wilt slightly. Crumble in the blue cheese at this stage.

5 Spread the filling evenly over the base of the tart case.

6 Beat the eggs, milk and cream together with the chopped parsley and seasoning in a bowl, then pour the mixture over the filling in the tart case. Bake in the oven for 25–30 minutes until the filling is set. Serve with a large salad.

PAN-FRIED DOVER SOLE WITH BUTTERED LEEKS AND CHAMPAGNE SAUCE

When cooked and served correctly, Dover sole is a sensational fish to behold. The champagne sauce takes a little bit of watching and concentration, but it is well worth the effort for a special-occasion treat. You can use a good sparkling wine as a more cost-effective alternative to the champagne, if you prefer.

SERVES 4

25g/1oz/¼ cup plain (all-purpose) flour

Salt and freshly ground black pepper

4 Dover sole on the bone, skinned

75g/3oz/¾ stick butter

A drizzle of sunflower oil

Juice of ½ lemon

BUTTERED LEEKS

50g/2oz/½ stick butter

3 large leeks, trimmed and thinly sliced

3 tbsp white wine

4 tbsp pouring cream

½ tsp wholegrain mustard

Salt and freshly ground black pepper

Ingredients continued →

1 Begin by making the buttered leeks. Melt the butter in a large frying pan, add the leeks and cook over a gentle heat for 3–4 minutes or until the leeks are becoming nice and soft. At this stage pour in the white wine and allow this to reduce for a moment or two then pour in the cream and stir in the mustard. Season to taste with salt and pepper.

2 To make the sauce, pour the champagne into a saucepan with the shallot, then bring to the boil and boil until reduced to less than half. Pass the champagne through a sieve (strainer) into a bowl and allow to cool slightly.

3 Place the egg yolks in a large heatproof bowl and add the slightly cooled champagne. Set the bowl over a saucepan of lightly simmering water and continue to whisk constantly and also ensuring that it does not turn into champagne-flavoured scrambled eggs. I normally take it on and off the heat to prevent it from becoming overcooked. Allow this to cook until the mixture turns a pale colour and then add the butter – very slowly and in small batches. Whisk in the butter, piece by piece, while continuing to take the bowl on and off the heat. When all the butter is added, whisk in the cream and the chives.

CHAMPAGNE SAUCE

1 snipe (200ml/7 fl oz/
  generous ¾ cup)
  champagne

1 shallot, peeled and very
  finely chopped

3 large free-range egg yolks

100g/3½oz/1 stick hard butter,
  cut into small pieces

50ml/2fl oz/¼ cup pouring
  cream

2 tsp chopped fresh chives

4 To cook the fish, place the flour on a large plate and season with a little salt and pepper. Dip the Dover sole into the seasoned flour and coat on both sides.

5 Meanwhile, heat a large frying pan with a little butter and tiny drizzle of oil and pan-fry the fish on both sides until they are golden brown, about 4 minutes on each side should be enough. If you need to, place the fish in an oven preheated to 180°C (350°F), Gas mark 4 for a few minutes while you are finishing off the sauce, but be careful not to overcook it. When cooked, the flesh should feel quite springy and willing to come away from the bone.

6 Just before serving, remove the fish from the bone. It is quite easy to do, but you must be careful with it. Use a sharp knife to cut right down the central bone and use a palette knife to slide in underneath each fillet to carefully lift it off the bone. Do the same on the other side of the fish. If you are careful you will be able to reassemble the fish (without the bone) back in its original form.

7 To serve, place the buttered leeks on serving plates with the sole then drizzle a small amount of the sauce around the fish.

ROASTED FILLET OF SALMON WITH SUN-DRIED TOMATO PESTO

I always think that salmon needs to be jazzed up a good bit, so in this recipe I pair it with a delicious Mediterranean-style pesto that gets spread on top of the salmon.

SERVES 4

4 salmon fillets, about 150g/5oz each

Salt and cracked black pepper

1 tbsp olive oil

Blanched asparagus spears, to serve

SUN-DRIED TOMATO PESTO

110g/4oz sun-dried tomatoes

Juice of ½ lemon

25g/1oz/¼ cup freshly grated Parmesan cheese

A large handful of fresh basil

3 garlic cloves, peeled and crushed

100ml/3½fl oz/scant ½ cup olive oil

Salt and freshly ground black pepper

1 Preheat the oven to 200°C (400°F), Gas mark 6.

2 Place the salmon in a roasting tray. Season with a little salt and cracked black pepper and drizzle the salmon with the olive oil. Roast in the oven for 12–14 minutes – this time will vary depending on the thickness of the fish.

3 To make the pesto, place the sun-dried tomatoes into a food processor with the other ingredients, including salt and pepper, and blitz until a coarse consistency is formed. If you would like the pesto a little thinner, you can add a little extra olive oil. Transfer the pesto to a container or jar and chill in the fridge until required. The pesto can be stored in the fridge for up to 2 weeks.

4 To serve, place the salmon on top of some spears of blanched asparagus and top with some of the sun-dried tomato pesto.

SMOKED TROUT
WITH POACHED EGGS
AND HOLLANDAISE SAUCE

The flavours in this dish are delicious together and the trout makes a nice change from smoked salmon. It's fantastic as a brunch option, or you could also turn it into a starter (appetizer). If you wish, the eggs and hollandaise can be prepared in advance, leaving you just the trout to cook at the last minute.

SERVES 6

I tsp white wine vinegar
6 eggs
Hollandaise Sauce, to serve
  (see page 195)

SMOKED TROUT

25g/1oz/¼ stick butter
6 smoked trout fillets
Juice of ½ lemon

1 To poach the eggs, bring a medium saucepan of water to the boil. Add the white wine vinegar, then reduce the heat and crack in the eggs (3 at a time). Simmer for 4–5 minutes until the whites of the egg are set and the yolk still a little soft.

2 If using the eggs later, then at this stage remove the eggs from the heat and transfer them into a bowl of cold water until you are ready to serve them later on. If you want to reheat them then pop them under a hot grill (broiler) or back into a saucepan of hot water.

3 Melt the butter in a large frying pan and quickly fry the trout fillets for 2–3 minutes on each side until they are gently cooked. If preferred, you could pop the trout under a preheated hot grill for about 3–4 minutes on each side. When the fish are almost cooked, sprinkle the trout with a little lemon juice.

4 Serve the pan-fried trout with a perfectly poached egg and a spoonful of hollandaise sauce.

SPICED FISH STEW

In Arthurstown, where we live, there is a huge variety of seafood and shellfish available, so I often get a selection to put in this stew. It's a much healthier option than a typical cream-based seafood chowder. Serve with a large bowl of crusty bread.

SERVES 6–8

A drizzle of sunflower oil

1 large onion, peeled and diced

3 garlic cloves, peeled and crushed

1 green chilli, finely diced

2.5cm/1in piece fresh root ginger (gingerroot), peeled and diced

2 celery sticks, diced

1 head of fennel, trimmed and sliced

1 leek, trimmed and thinly sliced

2 carrots, peeled and cut into cubes

1 sweet potato, peeled and cut into cubes

1 level tsp saffron strands

1 large glass white wine

1 x 400g tin (can) chopped tomatoes

2 tbsp crème fraîche

1 tsp fennel seeds

½ tsp ground cumin

600ml/1 pint/2½ cups well-flavoured fish stock (see page 205)

900g/2lb selection mixed fish (e.g. cod, salmon, monkfish, smoked haddock and brill)

450g/1lb live mussels, cleaned (see tip)

1 Heat a large heavy-based saucepan and add the oil. Add the onion, garlic, chilli and ginger and cook over a low heat for about 5 minutes until they have softened completely. Add the vegetables and allow them to cook gently for 5–10 minutes.

2 Place the saffron strands in a small bowl and cover with about 2 tablespoons of boiling water then add to the pan with the white wine and allow them to reduce by about half. Add the chopped tomatoes and crème fraîche and bring the mixture to the boil. Stir thoroughly.

3 At this stage sprinkle in the fennel seeds and ground cumin. Pour in the fish stock then reduce the heat and simmer for about 20 minutes. (The stew can be prepared up to this stage in advance.)

4 Chop the fish into very large chunks then add them, with the mussels, to the soup and allow them to poach in the liquor. This should take no longer than 5–6 minutes or until the mussels are open. Discard any mussels that do not open.

TIP

To clean mussels, rinse the mussels under cold running water then scrub the shells well to remove any grit and barnacles. Pull away the beard and tap any mussels that are open with the back of a knife or on the work surface (counter). If they don't close immediately, discard them. Rinse again before cooking.

PAN-FRIED JOHN DORY WITH WILD GARLIC AND CHERRY TOMATO VINAIGRETTE

This is a really lovely dish that uses a type of fish that I think people ought to cook more often. If you can't find John Dory, try tilapia or porgy instead. When wild garlic is not in season, you could replace with some fresh basil or spring onions (scallions).

SERVES 4

50g/2oz/½ stick butter

4 John Dory fillets, about 175g/6oz each

Salt and cracked black pepper

Minted new potatoes, to serve

WILD GARLIC AND CHERRY TOMATO VINAIGRETTE

Sunflower oil, for cooking

2 small shallots, peeled and thinly sliced

12–16 cherry tomatoes, left whole

Salt and cracked black pepper

1 small bunch of wild garlic leaves (when chopped about 3 tbsp)

Juice of 1 lemon

200ml/7fl oz/generous ¾ cup olive oil

1 tbsp capers

1 Begin by making the wild garlic and tomato vinaigrette. Heat a medium saucepan gently with a tiny amount of sunflower oil. Add the shallots and cook very gently for about 3 minutes until they are just softened but not entirely coloured. Next add the cherry tomatoes and pan-roast them for 2–3 minutes until they have softened and roasted. Season with a little salt and cracked black pepper at this stage. Mix in the chopped wild garlic leaves and wilt for 20–30 seconds until just softened. Turn off the heat now and pour in the lemon juice and olive oil then add the capers. Allow to stand for at least 15 minutes to allow the flavours to infuse.

2 Heat a large frying pan and add a little butter. Season the fish with salt and pepper and pan-fry for 2–3 minutes on each side or until just gently cooked.

3 Serve the pan-roasted fish on a serving platter, drizzled with the wild garlic and tomato vinaigrette and with minted new potatoes.

MEDITERRANEAN COD BAKE

———

This is a very simple main course (entrée) to prepare, and is also simple in terms of presentation as it can be served directly to the table. Baked fish is delicious because it tends to retain all of its moisture, and the baking process is an ideal method if you are nervous of cooking fish (which can be a precarious task) because it tends not to fall apart.

SERVES 6

Sunflower oil, for cooking

75g/3oz chorizo, diced into fairly small chunks

3 garlic cloves, peeled and diced

I red onion, peeled and diced into fairly small chunks

I red (bell) pepper, diced into fairly small chunks

I green (bell) pepper, diced into fairly small chunks

I courgette (zucchini), diced into fairly small chunks

150g/5oz/1¼ cups mushrooms, diced into fairly small chunks

I x 400g tin (can) chopped tomatoes

6 cod fillets

Salt and cracked black pepper

3 tbsp fresh white breadcrumbs

TO SERVE

Green salad

Boiled baby potatoes dressed with mint butter

I Preheat the oven to 190°C (375°F), Gas mark 5.

2 Heat a large frying pan with a little oil. Add the chorizo and garlic and cook for 3–4 minutes to allow the spiced flavour of the chorizo to flavour the oil. Add the vegetables and continue to cook for a further 4–5 minutes until they begin to soften. Next add the chopped tomatoes and allow these to bubble up for about 5–6 minutes.

3 Pour the vegetable mixture into a large casserole dish and lay the cod fillets on top. Season lightly with a little salt and pepper and scatter the breadcrumbs on top. Bake in the oven for 15–20 minutes (depending on the thickness of the fish).

4 Serve with a large green salad and boiled baby potatoes dressed with mint butter.

BRAISED CHICKEN WITH SMOKED BACON AND MUSHROOM GRAVY

At the end of a winter's day, it's lovely to come home to a warm and comforting stew or casserole. I like to use a full-bodied Burgundy in this recipe, but feel free to use your own favourite red.

SERVES 6

Sunflower oil, for cooking

6 chicken breasts, skin on

Salt and freshly ground black pepper

25g/1oz/¼ stick butter

6–8 shallots, peeled but left whole

8 mushrooms, sliced

4 rashers (slices) of bacon, roughly diced or 110g/4oz/ scant ½ cup smoked bacon lardons

25g/1oz /¼ cup plain (all-purpose) flour

½ glass red wine

1 tsp tomato purée (tomato paste)

900ml/1½ pints/3½ cups good-quality well-flavoured chicken stock (see page 203)

½ tsp wholegrain mustard (optional)

Vegetables and roasted potatoes, to serve

1 Heat a large saucepan with a little oil. Season the chicken breasts with a little salt and pepper then place the chicken in the pan and fry over a high heat for 3–4 minutes until lightly browned on all sides. Remove the chicken from the pan and set aside for a few moments while you make the sauce.

2 Preheat the oven to 180°C (350°F), Gas mark 4.

3 Melt the butter in the pan, add the shallots, mushrooms and bacon and cook for 5–6 minutes or until they are just beginning to colour. Sprinkle in the flour and stir until everything is coated in the flour. Carefully pour in the red wine then stir in the tomato purée. Add the stock at this stage. If you are using the wholegrain mustard, then add this now as well. Bring to a gentle boil, then reduce the heat and simmer for about 5 minutes until it has thickened.

4 Place the chicken in a casserole dish and pour the hot sauce over the chicken.

5 Cover the dish with a lid or foil and bake in the oven for 40–50 minutes. Uncover and bake for a further 15–20 minutes. Serve with some crisp vegetables and crunchy roasted potatoes.

TORTILLA WRAPS
WITH BARBECUED CAJUN CHICKEN
AND LIME DRESSING

This is a fresh, vibrant option for a quick midweek supper. Cajun chicken shouts barbecue, but if the weather is bad, the chicken can be cooked inside under the grill, and the wraps are just as delicious all year round to bring a hint of sunshine to your plate.

SERVES 8

4 chicken breasts, sliced

I heaped tsp Cajun spice

4 tsp sunflower oil

6 tortilla wraps

FILLINGS

Mixed salad leaves (salad greens)

8–12 cherry tomatoes, halved

½ cucumber, thinly sliced

2 red onions, peeled and sliced

LIME DRESSING

200ml/7fl oz/generous ¾ cup natural (plain) yoghurt

4 tsp olive oil

Finely grated zest and juice of I lime

Freshly ground black pepper

1 To make the lime dressing, combine all the ingredients together in a bowl and store in the fridge until required.

2 Preheat the barbecue (grill) or grill (broiler). Place the chicken in a large clean bowl and sprinkle the Cajun spice powder over the top. Add the oil and mix thoroughly to make sure that the chicken is fully coated with the spice mixture. Cook the chicken breasts for about 4 minutes on each side (depending on thickness) until they are cooked thoroughly.

3 Meanwhile, lay the tortilla wraps on the work surface (counter) and spread a spoonful of the dressing in the centre of each wrap. Put some mixed leaves, cherry tomatoes, cucumber and red onion on the wrap and add some of the cooked chicken. Roll each wrap up very tightly (like a Swiss roll/jelly roll). Serve as required.

PRESENTATION TIP

When the tortilla wrap has been rolled tightly, cut both ends off to even it then cut the remainder in half at an angle with a sharp knife. Place one half on the serving platter and stand the other half beside it. You may need to use a cocktail stick (toothpick) garnished with a cherry tomato at the end to secure the wrap in place.

MUM'S PERI PERI CHICKEN WITH CIDER

My mother lived in Rhodesia (now Zimbabwe) from the age of two until she was 18. I think it was there that she developed her great love of food and I have it to thank for the eclectic mix of cuisine that I enjoyed when I was growing up. Her Peri Peri chicken was a very popular choice and even now when she makes it the entire family gets excited! There are several different ways to make a Peri Peri marinade, most of which rely on fresh chillies, but mum prefers to use dried herbs and spices. Be warned: this dish is HOT!

SERVES 6

1 large chicken, jointed (or 6 chicken breasts)
6 garlic cloves, peeled and finely chopped
2 tsp chilli powder
½ tsp rock salt
1 tsp paprika
½ tsp dried oregano
1 tsp ground cumin
½ tsp ground coriander
A drizzle of olive oil
300ml/10floz/1¼ cups dry (hard) cider

TO SERVE

Large salad
Baked potatoes

1 Preheat the oven to 190°C (375°F), Gas mark 5.

2 Place the garlic in a mixing bowl, add the chilli powder, salt, paprika, oregano, cumin and coriander and mix well.

3 Place the chicken pieces in a large freezer bag and add the spice rub. Seal the bag and shake well to make sure that the chicken is well coated. Arrange the chicken pieces in a large roasting tin, drizzle with a little oil and bake in the oven for about 10–15 minutes.

4 Remove the chicken from the oven and pour the cider over the top. There is normally enough left to take a little sip!! Return the chicken to the oven and cook for a further 45–50 minutes, basting regularly, until the chicken is coated with a nice spicy glaze. If using chicken breasts, cook for just 25-30 minutes.

5 Serve with a large salad, baked potatoes and an optional bottle of cider!

ROAST CHICKEN WITH MUSHROOM AND COURGETTE STUFFING

As many of my readers will know, my all-time favourite dinner is roast chicken. This particular recipe, with its unusual stuffing, is one I developed quite recently and it has been very well received in Casa Dundon.

SERVES 6

75g/3oz/¾ stick butter, plus extra for the chicken

½ medium onion, peeled and diced

1 medium courgette (zucchini), diced

110g/4oz/¾ cup wild mushrooms, roughly torn

Finely grated zest of 1 lemon

2 tsp chopped fresh sage

200g/7oz/4 cups soft white breadcrumbs

Salt and cracked black pepper

1 large free-range chicken

1 Melt the butter in a medium saucepan, add the onion, courgette and wild mushrooms and cook over a very low heat for 5-6 minutes until all of these ingredients are softened completely. Mix in the lemon zest, the chopped sage and the breadcrumbs then season lightly and allow to cool.

2 Preheat the oven to 200°C (400°F), Gas mark 6.

3 Stuff the cavity of the chicken with the cold stuffing and secure the flap with a cocktail stick (toothpick). Place the chicken onto a roasting tray. Loosen the skin of the chicken and push a little extra butter under the skin and gently massage the butter into the chicken breasts. Sprinkle a little salt and cracked black pepper over the skin.

4 Roast the chicken in the oven for 20–25 minutes. At this stage reduce the oven temperature to 160°C (325°F), Gas mark 3 and cook for a further 1 hour or until the juices run clear from the chicken when the thickest part is pierced with a skewer or sharp knife. The flesh (particularly on the leg and thigh) should feel tender, indicating the bird is cooked.

OVEN-BAKED POUSSINS WITH WHITE WINE AND MUSHROOM SAUCE

Poussins (squab chickens) are very small young chickens. They are tender and quick to cook and rather attractive to serve because they are normally cooked and plated up whole.

SERVES 4

75g/3oz/¾ stick butter (at room temperature)

5 fresh sage leaves, plus extra to garnish

2 garlic cloves, peeled and thinly sliced

4 oven-ready poussins (squab chickens)

Sunflower oil, for drizzling

Salt and freshly ground black pepper

Boiled baby potatoes and broccoli or a green vegetable stir-fry, to serve

WHITE WINE AND MUSHROOM SAUCE

25g/1oz/¼ stick butter

2 garlic cloves, peeled and diced

1 shallot, peeled and thinly sliced

200g/7oz flat cap mushrooms, sliced

1 glass white wine

300ml/10fl oz/1¼ cups pouring cream

75g/3oz/¾ cup freshly grated Parmesan cheese

Chopped fresh parsley

1 Preheat the oven to 180°C (350°F), Gas mark 4.

2 Mix the butter, sage and garlic together in a mixing bowl. Loosen the skin around the neck of each poussin and push a little of the flavoured butter under until evenly spread over the breast.

3 Arrange the poussins on a large roasting tray. Drizzle over a little oil and season with a little salt and pepper. Roast in the oven for 40–45 minutes or until the poussins are completely tender and golden brown. Leave to rest in a warm place for at least 10 minutes.

4 To make the sauce, heat a medium saucepan with the butter. Add the garlic, shallot and mushrooms and quickly sauté for 2–3 minutes until they are softened. At this stage pour in the white wine and cream and bring the mixture to a slow boil. Add the grated Parmesan and mix thoroughly. This is the thickening agent of the sauce and it will give a beautifully smooth consistency.

5 Taste the sauce at this stage and add a little salt and pepper if required. Just before you are ready to serve, add the chopped parsley for a little added colour.

6 Arrange the poussins on a serving platter, drizzle with some white wine and mushroom sauce and serve with some boiled baby potatoes and broccoli or a green vegetable stir-fry.

CREAMY FOREST MUSHROOM, SPINACH AND CHICKEN PIE

This delicious pie could also be made as little individual pies by cooking the mixture in ovenproof ramekins or the cups of a muffin tray, and cutting the pastry into small lids using a deep biscuit (cookie) cutter.

SERVES 6

25g/1oz/¼ stick butter

Sunflower oil, for cooking

4 large skinless chicken breasts, diced

1 leek, trimmed and thinly sliced

3 garlic cloves, peeled and crushed

200g/7oz/1½ cups forest mushrooms, roughly torn

Salt and freshly ground black pepper

25g/1oz/¼ cup plain (all-purpose) flour

½ glass white wine

50g/2oz/½ cup grated Cheddar cheese

400ml/14fl oz/1¾ cups milk

50ml/2fl oz/¼ cup pouring cream (optional)

75g/3oz/2 cups fresh baby leaf spinach

1 sheet of ready-rolled puff pastry

EGG WASH

1 egg

2 tbsp milk

1 Preheat the oven to 190°C (375°F), Gas mark 5.

2 Heat a large shallow saucepan with the butter and a little bit of oil to stop the butter from burning. Add the chicken and cook for 4–5 minutes. Add the leek, garlic and mushrooms at this stage together with a little salt and pepper and cook for a further 5 minutes.

3 Sprinkle in the flour and stir until all the liquid has dried up then pour in the white wine and add the cheese and the milk. Bring the mixture to a gentle boil while stirring all the time. If you like, you could add a little cream as well. Simmer for 5–6 minutes. At the last minute, add the spinach and cook until wilted. Transfer the mixture to a large casserole dish and neatly arrange the pastry on top.

4 For the egg wash, mix the egg and milk together in a small bowl.

5 Brush the pastry lightly with a little egg wash and bake in the oven for about 30 minutes.

CHICKEN MARYLAND

Chicken Maryland is one of those recipes that has been around for ever. It has been changed and altered many times over the years, and every place seems to have its own version, but the fundamentals are more or less the same. My Chicken Maryland involves breaded chicken, pineapple fritters, a slice of bacon and some baked tomatoes – delicious!

SERVES 6

50g/2oz/⅓ cup plain (all-purpose) flour, seasoned with salt and pepper

I egg, lightly beaten

100ml/3½fl oz/scant ½ cup milk

150g/5oz/3 cups fresh white breadcrumbs

½ tsp Cajun spice

6 skinless chicken breasts

6 rashers (slices) of bacon

3 ripe tomatoes, halved

PINEAPPLE FRITTERS

150g/5oz/I cup plain (all-purpose) flour

½ tsp baking powder

A pinch of salt

I egg

100ml/3½fl oz/scant ½ cup milk

6 pineapple rings

Sunflower oil, for frying

Ingredients continued →

I To make the fritters, mix the flour, baking powder and salt together. Whisk in the egg and milk until a thick batter is formed. Allow to rest for about 10–15 minutes.

2 Dip the pineapple rings in the batter, making sure they are well coated.

3 Heat a large frying pan with a little oil and shallow-fry the rings on both sides until golden brown and the batter is crisp. Alternatively, use a deep-fat fryer. Remove the fritters with a slotted spoon and drain on kitchen paper (paper towels). Set aside until required.

4 Preheat the oven to 180°C (350°F), Gas mark 4.

5 Prepare three medium bowls, one with the seasoned flour, a second with the beaten egg and milk and a third with the breadcrumbs and Cajun spice.

6 Dip the chicken into the seasoned flour and shake off any excess flour then immerse it fully in the egg wash mixture and drain off the excess and then finally dip the chicken into the Cajun breadcrumb mixture until coated all over.

7 Meanwhile, heat a large pan and pan-fry the breaded chicken, in batches, over a low heat for about 3 minutes on

TO SERVE

Green salad

Garlic and Chive Butter (see
  page 114)

Crème fraîche or pouring
  cream, to garnish

either side until golden brown. Place the sealed chicken on a flat baking tray and pop it into the oven for about 20 minutes until cooked right through and the juices run clear when a knife is inserted into the centre. (When the chicken is fully cooked it should feel firm in the centre when pressed.)

8 About 10–12 minutes before the chicken is cooked, remove from the oven and lay a bacon rasher on top of each piece, then place the pineapple fritter on top of that and finish it off with a tomato half. If desired, you can secure the entire combination with a cocktail stick (toothpick). Return the chicken to the oven and continue to cook.

9 Serve the Chicken Maryland with a green salad and garlic and chive butter.

THAI COCONUT CHICKEN

This is a very fragrant way of cooking chicken. Although I have used chicken breasts in the recipe, it also works particularly nicely with chicken legs or thighs; just increase the cooking time a little.

SERVES 6

1 tsp cumin seeds

1 tsp mustard seeds

1 tsp coriander seeds

1 tsp turmeric

100ml/3½fl oz/scant ½ cup pouring cream

2 garlic cloves, peeled and finely diced

1 red chilli, seeds kept for added heat and finely diced

2.5cm/1in piece fresh root ginger (gingerroot), peeled and finely diced

6 chicken breasts, with skin

1 medium onion, peeled and diced

1 x 400ml tin (can) coconut milk

Freshly chopped coriander, for sprinkling (optional)

Boiled basmati rice, to serve

1 Heat a large wok (with no oil), add the cumin, mustard and coriander seeds and stir-fry over a medium heat for 2–3 minutes or until the seeds begin to pop a little (quite similar to popcorn). Mix in the turmeric, then remove from the heat and allow the mixture to cool.

2 Once the mixture has cooled, mix in the cream then transfer to a food processor or small blender, add the garlic, chilli and ginger and blitz to make a coarse marinade. Place the chicken in a shallow non-metallic dish and pour the marinade over the chicken. Cover and leave for at least a few minutes.

3 Heat a flameproof casserole dish, add the marinated chicken pieces (but not the marinade) in batches and cook until they are browned on all sides. Add the onion at this stage and cook for a few minutes until it is a nice apricot or terracotta colour, then add the marinade and the coconut milk. Bring the mixture to the boil then transfer to the oven and cook for 25 minutes or until the chicken is cooked through and the juices run clear when a knife is inserted into the centre. (When the chicken is fully cooked it should feel firm in the centre when pressed.)

4 Remove the chicken from the oven, sprinkle a few coriander leaves over the chicken, if desired, and serve with plain boiled basmati rice.

CHICKEN AND SMOKED BACON SPAGHETTI WITH GARLIC BREAD

Pasta dishes are so popular and convenient when it comes to midweek meals, and this one brings together some nice strong flavours to keep things interesting. You can use any vegetables, so feel free to experiment.

SERVES 8

350g/12oz spaghetti

Salt and freshly ground black pepper

Sunflower oil or butter, for cooking

3 skinless chicken breasts, diced

6 rashers (slices) of smoked bacon, diced

2 garlic cloves, peeled and chopped

1 red onion, peeled and thinly sliced

1 courgette (zucchini), thinly sliced

6 mushrooms, thinly sliced

1 x 400g tin (can) chopped tomatoes

100ml/3½fl oz/scant ½ cup pouring cream

2 tsp chopped fresh mixed herbs, such as parsley, sage, rosemary and thyme

GARLIC BREAD

8 small bread rolls

75g/3oz/¾ stick butter

2 garlic cloves, peeled and finely chopped

2 tsp chopped fresh parsley

Salt and freshly ground black pepper

1 To make the garlic bread, preheat the oven to 180°C (350°F), Gas mark 4.

2 Slice open each bread roll. Mix the butter, garlic, parsley and seasoning together and spread over the rolls. Place on a baking tray and bake in the oven for 7–10 minutes until crispy.

3 Cook the spaghetti in a large pan of boiling salted water according to the packet instructions. Drain and set aside until required.

4 Heat a large saucepan with a little oil or butter, add the chicken, bacon and garlic and cook over a low heat for 4–5 minutes until it is gently cooked. Next add the red onion and courgette together with the mushrooms. Cook the vegetables for about 5 minutes or until they are softened. Next add the chopped tomatoes. (I normally wash out the can with a little extra water and add this to the dish just to make sure that you get all of the goodness of the tomatoes into the dish. It will make a delicious sauce.)

5 Add the cream and bring the mixture to the boil. Add the mixed herbs and cooked spaghetti and toss around until the pasta is coated in the sauce, then allow the spaghetti to reheat thoroughly in the hot sauce. Adjust the seasoning accordingly and serve immediately with the crispy garlic bread.

HONEY AND MUSTARD CHICKEN SKEWERS

These attractive chicken skewers are extremely flavoursome. They are great for a summer barbecue or can be cooked under the grill (broiler) at other times of the year. If you wish, you could also use the marinade on whole chicken breasts.

SERVES 4–6

3 skinless chicken breasts, cut into small dice

1½ mixed (bell) peppers, such as red, green and yellow, diced

½ courgette (zucchini), diced

6 cherry tomatoes

MARINADE

Finely grated zest and juice of ½ lemon

2 tbsp runny honey

1 tsp wholegrain mustard

2 fresh thyme sprigs, chopped

2 garlic cloves, peeled and chopped

A pinch of cayenne pepper or paprika

4 tbsp sunflower oil

TO SERVE

Plain boiled rice

Green salad

EQUIPMENT

8–12 metal or wooden skewers

1 Begin by making the marinade. Put the lemon zest and juice in a large mixing bowl with the honey. Add the mustard, thyme, garlic, cayenne pepper and oil and whisk thoroughly until combined.

2 Make up the chicken skewers. I normally put about 5 pieces of chicken on each skewer and alternate them with a piece of vegetable in between each one. It is a great way of making the dish very colourful and attractive. I find that the metal skewers are best, as they tend to be firmer and stronger to hold the contents but also because the wooden skewers can tend to burn slightly. If you are using wooden skewers, soak them in cold water for at least 30 minutes to prevent burning. Sometimes it can be a good idea to cover all exposed wood with foil to prevent blackening.

3 Once the skewers are assembled, arrange in a large shallow non-metallic dish and pour the marinade over them. Cover and allow them to marinate in the fridge for at least 1 hour but longer if time permits.

4 Preheat the barbecue (grill) or grill (broiler). Remove the skewers from the marinade and cook for 4–5 minutes on each side until the chicken is golden brown and cooked all the way through to the centre. If you are concerned about whether or not the skewers are cooked then cut a piece of chicken in the centre to ensure it is cooked through.

5 Serve with rice and a green salad.

PAN-ROASTED DUCK
WITH CRUNCHY APPLE
AND WALNUT STUFFING

I think of duck as a great dinner party staple because it suggests to people that you've gone to a lot of effort to prepare a special meal. You can try adding apricots, hazelnuts or pine nuts to your stuffing for added texture. Somtimes I even add 100g/4oz mashed potato to vary the consistency.

SERVES 6

6 duck breasts

Salt and freshly ground
  black pepper

Finely grated zest of 1 orange

½ tbsp chopped fresh
  thyme

Sunflower oil, for cooking

2 tbsp runny honey

STUFFING

75g/3oz/¾ stick butter

½ medium onion, peeled
  and chopped

1 cooking apple, peeled and
  roughly diced

2 tbsp chopped mixed herbs,
  such as thyme, rosemary,
  parsley and sage

175g/6oz/3½ cups fresh white
  breadcrumbs

Ingredients ⟶
continued

1 Begin by making the stuffing. Melt the butter in a large pan, add the onion and diced apple and fry gently for 4–5 minutes. Add the chopped herbs, breadcrumbs, walnuts and salt and pepper to taste and stir until combined. Allow to cool.

2 Lay the duck breasts on a chopping board or serving plate and season with a little salt and pepper. Mix the orange zest and thyme together and rub onto the duck breasts. If you have the time, allow to marinate in the fridge for 1–2 hours.

3 When ready to cook the duck, make the red wine and plum reduction. Melt the butter in a large saucepan. Add the shallots, garlic, thyme and the plums and glaze quickly until they are beginning to soften slightly. Next add the sugar and allow this to melt and bubble up around the sides of the pan. This will give a nice sweet flavour to the sauce and will provide a nice accompaniment to the duck. Next reduce the heat to quite low and pour in the red wine, tomato purée and port. Bring to a gentle boil then lower the heat to medium and cook for about 15–20 minutes until it is reduced to a syrup-like sauce.

50g/2oz/½ cup walnuts, chopped

Salt and freshly ground black pepper

RED WINE AND PLUM REDUCTION

½ tbsp butter

2 shallots, peeled and sliced

3 garlic cloves, peeled and chopped

2 fresh thyme sprigs

75g/3oz fresh plums, stoned (pitted) and diced

75g/3oz/generous ⅓ cup (solidly packed) dark brown sugar

600ml/I pint/2½ cups red wine

I tsp tomato purée (tomato paste)

I½ tbsp good-quality port

4 Heat a large frying pan with a tiny amount of oil, add the duck and pan-fry quickly on both sides for 4–5 minutes until crispy and golden brown. Drizzle with a little honey and allow the honey to heat in the pan and glaze the duck breasts. Allow to rest for 5 minutes.

5 Serve the duck on top of the crunchy walnut stuffing. Pour a little of the red wine and plum reduction over the duck and serve the rest of the reduction in a jug (pitcher) separately.

TIP
The stuffing can be made in advance and frozen. It can also be used to stuff a whole chicken or some pork steaks. It's a great time saver for a Sunday roast!

CONFIT OF DUCK
WITH BRAISED RED CABBAGE

_____

The colours in this dish are absolutely fantastic. Confit is a fairly lengthy process, but it is well worth the effort for a special dinner party as duck always goes down brilliantly with guests.

SERVES 6

6 large duck legs

110g/4oz sel gris or rock salt

900g/2lb duck fat or goose fat

Frisée lettuce, to serve

BRAISED RED CABBAGE

450g/1lb red cabbage, cored and thinly sliced

1 onion, peeled and thinly sliced

250g/9oz cooking apples, peeled, cored and sliced

1½ tbsp white wine vinegar

1½ tbsp light muscovado sugar

¼ tsp mixed ground spices, such as cloves, nutmeg and cinnamon

½ tsp salt

Freshly ground black pepper

15g/½oz/⅛ stick butter

1 Make the duck confit at least 24 hours before you want to serve this dish. Place one duck leg in the bottom of a deep plastic, glass or stainless-steel bowl, sprinkle with a little of the salt, turn it over, sprinkle with more salt and add another duck leg. Continue until you've used up the duck legs and the salt. Cover and leave in the fridge for 6 hours, turning the legs over halfway through. Don't leave any longer or the duck will become too salty.

2 Preheat the oven to 140°C (275°F), Gas mark 1.

3 Rub the salt off the duck legs and pat them dry with kitchen paper (paper towels). Bring the duck or goose fat to a gentle simmer in a casserole dish in which the duck legs will fit snugly. Add the legs, making sure they are completely submerged, cover and transfer the dish to the oven. Cook for 1½ hours then remove from the oven and allow to cool in the fat. Chill for at least 24 hours or until needed.

4 For the braised red cabbage, preheat the oven to 150°C (300°F), Gas mark 2.

5 Arrange the cabbage, onion, apples, vinegar, sugar and spices in layers in a small casserole dish, season with the salt and pepper, dot with butter and cover with a well-fitting lid. Cook in the oven for 3 hours, stirring once or twice.

6 To serve, you can reheat the duck in one of two ways. Preheat the oven to 220°C (425°F), Gas mark 7. Lift the duck legs out of the fat and wipe off most but not quite all of it with kitchen paper (paper towels). Put them skin-side up onto a rack resting over a roasting tin and roast for 15–20 minutes until the skin is crisp and golden and the meat has heated through. Alternatively, sauté the legs in a frying pan over a medium heat until crisp, golden and heated through. Either way, they are delicious.

7 Spoon some of the red cabbage slightly to one side of six warm plates and rest a piece of the duck confit on top. Serve with frisée lettuce.

TIP
The red cabbage can be made in advance and reheated as required. It's also delicious with some added diced pears, prunes or apricots.

KEVIN'S PERFECT BURGER

Everybody you meet has a different recipe for the ideal burger. My preferred method includes two of my favourite flavours – cinnamon and mustard. I often have some of these burgers kept in the freezer for an impromptu summer barbecue.

SERVES 8

Sunflower oil, for cooking

1 red onion, peeled and finely chopped

900g/2lb minced (ground) beef, ideally rump or chuck steak

1 heaped tsp ground cumin

1 heaped tsp ground coriander

1 heaped tsp ground cinnamon

1 large egg

50g/2oz/½ cup freshly grated Parmesan cheese

1 tsp Dijon mustard

RELISH (OPTIONAL)

225g/8oz tomatoes, chopped

100ml/3½fl oz/scant ½ cup white wine vinegar

50g/2oz/¼ cup caster sugar

1 red chilli, chopped

3–4 allspice berries, crushed

TO SERVE

6 fine slices of cheese

6 white buns, lightly toasted

Lettuce leaves (greens)

Tomato slices

Sliced gherkins

1 Heat a little oil in a small frying pan, add the red onion and fry gently, stirring frequently, for about 5 minutes until softened.

2 Transfer the onion to a large bowl, add the minced beef, cumin, coriander and cinnamon and, using your hands, mix together. Break in the egg and mix in. Add the Parmesan and Dijon mustard and mix well.

3 Shape the mince mixture into 8 even-sized patties and place on a plate. Cover and chill in the fridge for about 2–3 hours until firm. The burgers won't keep chilled for longer than 12 hours but can be frozen for up to 3 months.

4 While the burgers are chilling, make the relish, if desired. Place the tomatoes, vinegar, sugar, chilli and allspice in a heavy-based saucepan. Bring to the boil, then reduce the heat and simmer, stirring now and then, until reduced and thickened to a jam-like consistency, about 20 minutes. Allow to cool.

5 Grill or fry the burgers. If grilling, preheat a barbecue (grill) and cook the burgers on a medium hot barbecue for 5 minutes on each side then allow to rest on a cooler part of the barbecue to allow them to finish cooking through to the centre. Use a knife to check they are fully cooked.

Continued ⟶

6 To fry the burgers, heat a large frying pan with a tiny amount of oil and cook the burgers over a medium heat for 4–5 minutes then turn them over and cook for a further 4–5 minutes. The burgers should feel quite firm when sufficiently cooked. If they are very thick you can finish cooking them in the oven.

7 Remove the freshly cooked burgers from the heat and top each with a slice of cheese, allowing the cheese to melt with the heat from the piping hot burger. Serve the burgers in lightly toasted white buns with layers of lettuce, sliced tomato and sliced gherkins, with the tomato relish, if desired.

TIP
These burgers are equally delicious made with minced lamb

ALTERNATIVE TOPPINGS:
- Slices of crispy bacon
- Slices of cucumber
- Sweet chilli mayonnaise
- Blue cheese

PAN-SEARED FILLET OF BEEF WITH GLAZED SHALLOTS AND BACON LARDONS

This is a meal that we often have at home for Sunday lunch. There is something very special about the smell of smoked bacon cooking and here it marries very well with the flavour of the beef. Instead of potatoes, I like to serve this with rösti, though I prefer to make several small röstis rather than one large one. The glazed shallots are a nice accompaniment or garnish and can also be served with many other recipes.

SERVES 4

1 handful of fresh rosemary and thyme sprigs

2 bay leaves

3–4 black peppercorns

5 tbsp sunflower oil

4 beef fillets (tenderloin), about 200g/7oz each

15g/½oz/⅛ stick butter

8–12 shallots, peeled and halved

6–8 rashers (slices) of smoked bacon, diced

3 garlic cloves, peeled and chopped (optional)

Salt and freshly ground black pepper

POTATO ROSTI

3 large potatoes

Salt and freshly ground black pepper

50g/2oz/½ stick butter

1 It is important to marinate the beef first. Put the rosemary, thyme and bay leaves into a large bowl with the black peppercorns. Pour the oil onto the herbs and mix around thoroughly. Place the beef into the marinade, cover and allow to marinate in the fridge for up to 2 hours or preferably overnight.

2 Heat a pan until it is very hot – there is no need to add any additional oil as the marinade covering the beef is enough. Seal the beef on both sides for about 3 minutes on each side (or a little more or less depending on how you like your beef cooked). Remove the pan from the heat and allow to rest for a couple of minutes then slice to serve.

3 To make the potato rösti, peel and grate the potatoes and put them into a large bowl. Season with salt and pepper and mix well.

Continued ⟶

4 Heat a large deep frying pan with the butter. Arrange spoonfuls of the potato mixture in the pan and cook gently for about 2 minutes. Carefully flip over and cook for a further 2 minutes. When they are cooked, they should be crisp and dry. Repeat this process for any remaining cakes.

5 For the glazed shallots and bacon lardons accompaniment, melt the butter in a pan and add the shallots together with the diced bacon. Cook over quite a high heat for 3–4 minutes until they are crispy and golden brown. If you wish, you could add a little garlic to the pan.

6 To serve, arrange the röstis on individual serving plates, place the sliced beef on top and pile the glazed shallots and bacon lardons on top.

STEAK SANDWICH WITH FLAT CAP MUSHROOMS AND GARLIC AND CHIVE BUTTER

A good steak is always a must at a barbecue. I believe the real secret is not to complicate the steak with excessive or unnecessary flavours.

SERVES 6

6 x strip loin steaks (New York steaks), about 225g/8oz each

3–4 fresh rosemary sprigs

1 head of garlic

5–6 black peppercorns

2 bay leaves

200ml/7fl oz/generous ¾ cup olive oil

4 tsp balsamic vinegar (optional)

Bread rolls, to serve

GARLIC AND CHIVE BUTTER

175g/6oz/1½ sticks butter, softened

3 garlic cloves, peeled and crushed

4 tsp snipped fresh chives

TO GARNISH

6 flat cap mushrooms, peeled

Sunflower oil, for brushing

Salt and freshly ground black pepper

1 To make the garlic and chive butter, mix all the ingredients together in a bowl and store in the fridge until required. It can be frozen if desired.

2 Cut the steaks into desired portions – try not to cut them too thick, then lay the steaks out flat in a large dish and scatter the dry ingredients over them. There is no need to peel the head of garlic, just chop it up quite roughly.

3 Cover with the olive oil and balsamic vinegar, if using, then cover and allow to rest in the fridge for at least a couple of hours. Because this is a mildly flavoured marinade, you can leave it for 2–3 days.

4 Heat the barbecue (grill) or grill (broiler) and cook for 2 minutes on each side for rare, 4 minutes on each side for medium and 5 minutes on each side for well done. Try not to over-agitate the steaks while they are cooking on the barbecue, instead just turn them once.

5 To make the garnish, brush the mushrooms lightly with oil and season with a pinch of salt and pepper. Place on the barbecue (grill) or on a hot plate and cook for 4–5 minutes until tender. Toast some bread rolls and serve with the mushrooms, steak and garlic and chive butter.

RICH BEEF
AND ROOT VEGETABLE
CASSEROLE

There is something very comforting about this rich beef dish. It is ideal for home entertaining and, as with lots of casserole-style dishes, it is even better the next day. If you are dicing the beef yourself then first trim off the fat to prevent the meat becoming tough during cooking.

SERVES 6–8

50g/2oz/½ stick butter

900g/2lb diced stewing beef

2 fresh rosemary sprigs

1 bouquet garni

3 large carrots, peeled and diced

200g/7oz turnips, peeled and diced

16 pearl onions, peeled

6 garlic cloves, peeled and diced

50g/2oz/⅓ cup plain (all-purpose) flour

1 large glass red wine

3 tbsp red wine vinegar

1 litre/1¾ pints/4 cups beef stock (see page 202)

1½ tbsp brandy (optional)

4 tsp tomato purée (tomato paste)

2 tsp redcurrant jelly

4 tbsp chopped fresh parsley

Boiled basmati rice and Garlic Bread (see page 100), to serve

1 Preheat the oven to 160°C (325°F), Gas mark 3.

2 Heat a large heavy-based frying pan with the butter and fry the beef in batches, until browned all over. Transfer to a large casserole dish and add the rosemary sprigs and bouquet garni.

3 Add the carrots, turnips, onions and garlic to the pan in which you browned the beef and cook for about 2 minutes or until they are all nicely browned. Sprinkle in the flour and stir until all the vegetables are coated in the flour and any juices that are left behind by the beef have dried up. Pour in the red wine, wine vinegar, stock and brandy, if using, then stir in the tomato purée and redcurrant jelly. Bring the mixture to the boil then pour over the beef in the casserole dish and cover with a lid. Cook in the oven for up to 2 hours until the meat is nice and tender.

4 Remove the casserole from the oven and sprinkle the chopped parsley over the top. Delicious served with plain boiled basmati rice and a big chunk of garlic bread.

BOBOTIE

This was declared the national dish of South Africa by the United Nations women's organisation in 1954. It has a varied heritage – the Dutch brought minced (ground) meat to local cuisine, the spices were introduced by slaves from Indonesia and the presentation is reminiscent of English Shepherd's Pie. My mother was a tremendous cook and this dish was always a firm favourite of hers; it was her method of using up the leftovers from Sunday lunch.

SERVES 6–8

2 slices of bread

200ml/7fl oz/generous ¾ cup milk

1 tbsp sunflower oil

2 medium onions, peeled and finely chopped

1 tsp crushed garlic

1 tsp freshly grated root ginger (gingerroot)

½ tbsp curry powder

1 tsp turmeric

900g/2lb minced (ground) beef or lamb

2 tbsp brown sugar

1 tbsp tomato chutney

Juice of ½ lemon

75g/3oz/½ cup raisins

Salt and freshly ground black pepper

TOPPING

2 large eggs

200ml/7fl oz/generous ¾ cup milk (reserved from soaking the bread)

1 Preheat the oven to 170°C (325°F), Gas mark 3.

2 Soak the bread in the milk for about 10 minutes, then strain, reserving the milk, and fluff the bread up with a fork.

3 Heat the oil in a frying pan, add the onions and sauté until soft. Add the garlic, ginger, curry powder and turmeric and mix quickly to coat the onions in the spice. Add the beef and continue to stir over a medium heat until browned.

4 Add the sugar, mashed bread, chutney, lemon juice and raisins to the mixture in the pan and season with salt and pepper. Spoon the mixture into a casserole dish and bake in the oven for 35 minutes.

5 For the topping, mix the eggs and the reserved milk together then remove the casserole from the oven and pour the egg mixture on top of the meat. Season with cracked black pepper and bake for a further 15–20 minutes.

CREAMY BEEF
AND MUSHROOM STROGANOFF

This dish is great on cold, wet evenings, as it is instantly warming and nourishing for all the family.

SERVES 6

25g/1oz/¼ stick butter

2 tsp sunflower oil

600g/1lb 5oz beef fillet (tenderloin), sliced into thin strips

½ tsp paprika or cayenne pepper

225g/8oz/scant 2 cups mixed wild mushrooms, torn

2 shallots, peeled and diced

1 garlic clove, peeled and crushed

3½ tbsp brandy

250ml/9fl oz/1 cup soured cream

Salt and freshly ground black pepper

TO SERVE

Chopped flat-leaf parsley (optional)

Boiled basmati rice

1 Heat a large heavy-based frying pan with the butter and oil.

2 Place the beef in a large bowl, add the paprika or cayenne and mix into the beef. Mix the beef around to make sure that it is fully coated. Add the beef to the hot pan and fry quickly until it is browned all over. Mix in the mushrooms, diced shallots and garlic and cook for 3–4 minutes until they are softened.

3 Pour in the brandy and allow this to ignite (first turn off your overhead extractor fan) and allow the alcohol to evaporate off.

4 Next pour in the soured cream and bring the mixture to the boil. Reduce the heat and simmer for 3–4 minutes until the sauce has sufficiently reduced. Season to taste with salt and pepper and serve with some chopped parsley, if desired, and plain boiled basmati rice.

TIP
Sliced gherkins can be added at the last minute for flavour and as a garnish.

ROASTED RIB OF BEEF
WITH GLAZED ROOT VEGETABLES AND HORSERADISH CREAM

———

Sunday lunches have always been a real tradition in our home. Rib of beef is one of my favourite Sunday roasts. I think that the flavour of the meat cooked on the bone is far superior to when it is cooked off it. The addition of the horseradish cream finishes this dish off wonderfully well.

SERVES 6–8

2kg/4lb 6oz rib of beef on the bone

Salt and freshly ground black pepper

25g/1oz/⅛ cup duck fat

3 large carrots, peeled and roughly chopped

2 large parsnips, peeled and roughly chopped

1 large turnip, peeled and roughly chopped

1 courgette (zucchini), roughly chopped

25g/1oz/¼ stick butter

1 tbsp chopped mixed herbs, such as rosemary and thyme

HORSERADISH CREAM

4 tsp grated horseradish

4 tsp white wine vinegar

½ tsp Dijon mustard

A pinch of caster (superfine) sugar

Salt and freshly ground black pepper

225ml/8fl oz/scant 1 cup whipping cream, lightly whipped

1 To make the horseradish cream, simply mix all the ingredients together and store in a clean jar or serving bowl. Keep in the fridge when not in use. It can be stored for up to 2 days.

2 Preheat the oven to 190°C (375°F), Gas mark 5.

3 Place the beef on a large roasting tray. Sometimes I use some halved onions as a trivet to raise the meat slightly so it doesn't sit in its own juices. Season the meat lightly and rub in the duck fat.

4 Roast the meat in the oven for 15–20 minutes per 450g/1lb for medium beef. If you would like the beef well done, leave it in for an additional 10 minutes per 450g/1lb then allow to rest for at least 15 minutes prior to carving.

5 Meanwhile, par-boil all the vegetables (with the exception of the courgette) for 5–6 minutes in a saucepan of lightly salted water until just tender, then drain and set aside.

6 Heat a large frying pan with the butter. Add the par-boiled root vegetables and courgettes and cook for 5–10 minutes or until they are all quite tender and well browned. The butter will assist in browning the vegetables. Add the chopped herbs just before serving the vegetables.

7 Arrange the vegetables onto a serving platter and carve the meat and arrange on top. Serve with the horseradish cream.

FILLET STEAKS ON SMOKED GUBEEN MASHED POTATO

Fillet of beef is one of my favourite dinner party treats. The flavour of the smoked cheese works really well with the mashed potato, but if you wish you could mash in a little pesto or tapenade (see pages 208 and 210) instead for a different flavour.

SERVES 6

6 fillet steaks (tenderloin), about 200g/7oz each

3–4 fresh rosemary sprigs

I head of garlic

5–6 black peppercorns

2 bay leaves

250ml/9fl oz/I cup olive oil

4 tsp balsamic vinegar (optional)

Crisp green beans, to serve

SMOKED GUBEEN MASHED POTATO

6 large floury (mealy) potatoes (Roosters are ideal)

50ml/2fl oz/¼ cup milk

25g/Ioz/¼ stick butter

A little pouring cream (optional)

75g/3oz/¾ cup smoked gubeen cheese, grated (other smoked cheese also works well)

I tbsp snipped fresh chives

Salt and freshly ground black pepper

I Begin by preparing the steaks. Cut the steaks into desired portions (if you do not have the luxury of a friendly butcher) then lay them out flat in a large dish and scatter the dry ingredients over them. There is no need to peel the garlic – just chop it quite roughly. Cover with the olive oil and balsamic vinegar if using, and leave to rest for at least a couple of hours. Because this is a mildly flavoured marinade, you can leave it for 2–3 days.

2 To make the mashed potato, peel the potatoes and cut into small chunks then cook in a saucepan of boiling water until tender. Drain and return the potatoes to the pan.

3 Warm the milk in the microwave or in a small saucepan, then mash the potatoes using the butter, warmed milk and a little cream, if using, until they are quite smooth and a piping consistency. Mix in the grated cheese and snipped chives and mix well until the cheese is melted. Season and keep warm until required.

4 To cook the steaks, heat a griddle pan (grill pan) or frying pan and cook to your liking – 2 minutes on each side for rare, 4 minutes on each side for medium and 5 minutes on each side for well done. Try not to over-agitate the meat while it is cooking, instead turning it just once. Allow the meat to rest for 5–10 minutes.

5 Serve the steak on top of the mashed potato and crisp green beans on the side.

BRAISED LAMB SHANKS
WITH CREAMY GARLIC POTATOES

Cheaper cuts of meat have really come back into vogue lately and the shank is one of my favourite parts of the lamb. The beauty of lamb shanks is that you can leave them braising away and they don't spoil if they are left to cook for a little longer than required. In the spring you could add some freshly chopped wild garlic to the potatoes instead of the roasted garlic bulb.

SERVES 6

Sunflower oil, for cooking

6 lamb shanks

25g/1oz/¼ stick butter

3 carrots, peeled and cut into large chunks

225g/8oz turnips, peeled and cut into large chunks

4 celery sticks, roughly sliced

4 garlic cloves, peeled and chopped

18 pearl onions, peeled

50g/2oz/⅓ cup plain (all-purpose) flour, seasoned with salt and pepper

1 tsp tomato purée (tomato paste)

125ml/4fl oz/½ cup red wine

500ml/18fl oz/2 cups lamb or chicken stock (see page 203)

1 bay leaf

1 bunch of fresh thyme

2–3 fresh rosemary sprigs

Chopped fresh parsley, to garnish

Ingredients continued ⟶

1 Preheat the oven to 150°C (300°F), Gas mark 2.

2 Heat a large deep pan with a little oil and fry the lamb shanks in batches until they are browned on all sides. Remove from the pan and transfer to a large casserole dish.

3 Add the butter to the pan and melt, then add the carrots, turnips, celery, garlic and pearl onions. Cook for 3–4 minutes until they are glazed. This will help to give the vegetables a nice lamb flavour. Sprinkle the flour into the pan and stir around until all the vegetables are coated in the flour and the juices have dried up. Stir in the tomato purée, then pour in the wine and stock and bring to the boil. Pour the sauce onto the lamb shanks in the casserole dish, add the bay leaf, thyme and rosemary and bake in the oven for 2–2½ hours until the meat is very soft and falling off the bone.

4 Make the creamy garlic potatoes while the lamb is in the oven. Roast the garlic in the oven for 30 minutes then squeeze out the pulp.

CREAMY GARLIC POTATOES

1 head garlic, unpeeled

6–8 potatoes

Salt and freshly ground black pepper

5 Peel the potatoes and cut into small chunks then cook in a saucepan of boiling water until tender. Drain and return the potatoes to the pan and mash with the garlic. Season to taste with salt and pepper.

6 Remove the casserole from the oven and make sure the meat is tender, if not, return to the oven for a few more minutes. Remove the meat from the casserole dish and, if required, boil the liquid in a saucepan on the hob until reduced or thickened.

7 Return the lamb to the sauce and serve alongside the potatoes, garnished with chopped parsley.

GAME PIE

There is something rich and opulent about a game pie. For the ultimate pie crust, I use a rich suet pastry, but you could alternatively use a ready-rolled all-butter puff pastry if you're short on time.

SERVES 6–8

Sunflower oil or butter

900g/2lb mixed selection of game meat

5 smoked bacon rashers (slices), diced

2 large onions, peeled and diced

225g/8oz/1¾ cups mixed wild mushrooms

3 garlic cloves, peeled and chopped

3 fresh thyme sprigs

2 heaped tbsp plain (all-purpose) flour

700ml/1¼ pints/3 cups well-flavoured game or chicken stock (see page 203)

1 glass red wine

3½ tbsp port

1 tsp tomato purée (paste)

Green salad, to serve

SUET PASTRY

225g/8oz/1½ cups plain (all-purpose) flour, plus extra for dusting

Salt and freshly ground black pepper

110g/4oz/¾ cup shredded suet

EGG WASH

1 egg

2 tbsp milk

1 Begin by making the pastry. Sift the plain flour into a large mixing bowl and add to it a little salt and pepper. Add the shredded suet and, using the back of a knife, mix it together well. Pour in enough cold water to bind it together. Pour in the water just a little at a time. You do not need to add too much water, so proceed with caution. Once the pastry has come together into a ball, transfer it to a well-floured work surface (counter) and knead for a few moments. Cover the pastry with clingfilm (plastic wrap) and allow to rest in the fridge for 1 hour.

2 Heat a large heavy-based pan with a little oil or butter. Add the game and bacon, in batches, and fry quite quickly until browned on all sides. Add the onions, mushrooms, garlic and thyme and fry until browned. Sprinkle in the flour and stir until the meat and vegetables are coated in the flour. Pour in the stock at this stage together with the red wine, port and tomato purée and bring the mixture to the boil. Reduce the heat and simmer for 2½ hours or until the meat is tender.

3 Preheat the oven to 190°C (375°F), Gas mark 5.

4 For the egg wash, mix the egg and milk together and set aside.

5 Transfer the game mixture to a large casserole dish. Roll out the rested pastry on a well-floured work surface and place on top of the game mixture in the casserole dish. Lightly brush the pastry with a little egg wash and bake for 25–30 minutes or until golden brown and bubbling. Serve with a green salad.

LAMB SKEWERS
WITH GREEK YOGHURT RELISH

Many people associate lamb with summer barbecues. This is the perfect recipe for just such an occasion, but it can also be cooked in the oven at other times of the year. The marinade works equally well on a butterflied leg of lamb if you want a variation.

SERVES 8–10

900g/2lb leg of lamb

Sunflower oil, for brushing

Green salad, to serve

MARINADE

150ml/5fl oz/⅔ cup natural (plain) yoghurt

1 tsp ground cumin

1 tsp ground coriander

2 garlic cloves, peeled and diced

Finely grated zest of 1 lemon

4 tsp chopped fresh coriander (cilantro)

GREEK YOGHURT RELISH

200ml/7fl oz/generous ¾ cup Greek yoghurt

2 tsp chopped fresh mint

2 garlic cloves, peeled and crushed

Juice of ½ lemon

Cracked black pepper

EQUIPMENT

16–20 wooden or metal skewers

1 If using wooden skewers, soak them in cold water for at least 30 minutes before using, to prevent them burning during cooking.

2 Dice the lamb into even-sized 2.5cm/1in cubes.

3 To make the marinade, mix the natural yoghurt, ground spices, diced garlic, lemon zest and coriander together. Carefully thread the lamb onto metal or soaked wooden skewers and lay them in a shallow non-metallic dish. Pour the marinade over the skewers and mix them around to make sure that the lamb is fully coated with the marinade. Cover and allow to marinate in the fridge for up to 3 hours, but preferably overnight if time allows.

4 Meanwhile, prepare the yoghurt relish to serve with your lamb skewers. Mix the yoghurt, mint, garlic and lemon juice together with the cracked black pepper. Set aside in the fridge until required.

5 To cook the lamb skewers, heat the barbecue (grill) and brush the bars carefully with a little oil. Place the skewers on the barbecue and cook for 2–3 minutes on all sides until the kebabs (kabobs) are cooked through. Alternatively, cook the skewers in an oven preheated to 200°C (400°F), Gas mark 6 for 15 minutes.

6 Serve the lamb skewers with a large green salad and some of the yoghurt relish.

MUSTARD-CRUSTED RACK OF LAMB

Rack of lamb is readily available from the butchers, but many people aren't sure what to do with it. This recipe is quite straightforward and ideal if you've never cooked a rack of lamb before. Despite its simplicity, if you are looking for a recipe to impress, look no further!

SERVES 6

6 individual racks of lamb, about 2–3 bones each, Frenchtrimmed

4 tsp Dijon mustard

2 tbsp chopped fresh parsley

110g/4oz/2 cups fresh white breadcrumbs

25g/1oz/¼ cup plain (all-purpose) flour

½ tsp tomato purée (tomato paste)

100ml/3½fl oz/scant ½ cup red wine

350ml/12fl oz/1½ cups beef stock (see page 202)

½ tsp chopped fresh rosemary leaves

A few handfuls of fresh redcurrants (optional)

Salt and freshly ground black pepper

1 Preheat the oven to 200°C (400°F), Gas mark 6.

2 When you are ordering the lamb, ask the butcher to French trim them for you. This peels all the fat off the bones and leaves the bones exposed. With a palette knife spread the mustard over the racks of lamb.

3 Mix the parsley and breadcrumbs together or blend in a food processor if you wish, then press the breadcrumb mixture on top of the mustard-coated racks.

4 Transfer the lamb to a roasting tray and bake in the oven for 18–20 minutes, depending on how you like your meat cooked. Remove from the oven, then take the lamb out of the roasting tray and allow to rest for 5 minutes. Carve as required.

5 While the lamb is resting, make the gravy. Remove the grease from the roasting tray, then put the roasting tray over a medium heat on the hob. Sprinkle in the flour and mix quickly until the flour gets a nice dark brown colour. Turn down the heat a little and mix in the tomato purée thoroughly. Pour in the red wine and stock and whisk continuously as the mixture begins to thicken. Bring to the boil, then strain the mixture into a clean saucepan and boil for 4–5 minutes to reduce. Add the rosemary to the gravy at this stage. If you wish, you could throw a few handfuls of fresh redcurrants into the pan as well. Season lightly.

6 To serve, slice the rack of lamb into individual cutlets, arrange on serving plates and drizzle with the gravy.

ROAST STUFFED PORK WITH ROAST POTATOES AND APPLE COMPOTE

I cook pork steaks quite often at home, and I've found a few clever ways to keep the meat nice and moist. Stuffing the pork is one such technique, and this stuffing does the job and is also quite delicious. The roast potatoes and apple compote are the classic accompaniments for a great pork roast.

SERVES 4–6

175g/6oz/3½ cups white breadcrumbs

½ medium onion, peeled and finely diced

Finely grated zest of 1 orange

1 eating apple, peeled, cored and grated

50g/2oz/⅓ cup sultanas (golden raisins)

2 tbsp fresh chopped parsley, thyme and chives

Sea salt and freshly ground pepper

75g/3oz/¾ stick butter, melted

1 large pork fillet (tenderloin)

3 rashers (slices) of bacon (optional)

Sunflower oil, for drizzling

6 potatoes, peeled

3 large fresh rosemary sprigs, to garnish

APPLE COMPOTE

5 large cooking apples, peeled, cored and diced

50g/2oz/¼ cup granulated sugar

1 Preheat the oven to 190°C (375°F), Gas mark 5.

2 Put the breadcrumbs, diced onion, orange zest, grated apple, sultanas, herbs and salt and pepper to taste into a large bowl and mix well. Add the melted butter and stir well. The stuffing should be soft and well bound together without being wet.

3 Clean the pork fillet well, removing the sinew and fat. Make a horizontal slit in the pork fillet to open it up, but don't cut all the way through. Make a few more slits in the pork to assist in flattening it out then use a rolling pin to flatten the meat.

4 Place the stuffing over the flattened fillet and roll it up tightly. If desired you can secure it with cocktail sticks (toothpicks) or bacon rashers. Place in a roasting tray, drizzle with a little oil and cover the meat loosely with foil. Cut the potatoes in half, place them in the tray around the pork and sprinkle with rosemary. Roast in the oven for 45–60 minutes. Remove the foil for the last 15 minutes of cooking. Remove from the oven and allow the meat to rest for at least 10–15 minutes before slicing.

5 Meanwhile, make the apple compote. Place the apples in a saucepan with the sugar and 4–5 tablespoons of water and cook over a low heat for 5–6 minutes. Turn off the heat and leave to rest in the pan for a further 10 minutes then, if desired, mash the apples roughly. Serve the apple compote alongside the pork.

CURRIED PORK MEATBALLS

Delicious and easy-to-make pork meatballs simmered in a chunky curry sauce. There's no need to buy loads of spices; you simply need a good red curry paste. It's a warming, nourishing dish, with just enough spice.

SERVES 6–8

900g/2lb minced (ground) pork

I red onion, peeled and finely chopped

75g/3oz/1½ cups fresh white breadcrumbs

I large bunch of fresh coriander (cilantro), chopped, plus extra

I tsp dried chilli flakes

2.5cm/1in piece fresh root ginger (gingerroot), peeled and finely chopped

2 garlic cloves, peeled and crushed

2 large egg yolks

I large apple, peeled and grated

½ tsp ground cumin

Sunflower oil, for drizzling

SAUCE

A drizzle of sunflower oil

I onion, peeled and diced

2 garlic cloves, peeled and chopped

2.5cm/1in piece fresh root ginger, peeled and chopped

2 tbsp red curry paste

I x 400g tin (can) chopped tomatoes

I x 400ml tin (can) coconut milk

Salt and freshly ground black pepper

1 Begin by making the meatballs. This process is very simple as you just put all of the ingredients apart from the oil together in a large mixing bowl and mash them together. It is vitally important that all of the ingredients are well incorporated into the mixture.

2 Using floured hands, divide and roll the mixture into small meatballs – the mixture should yield between 15–20 meatballs, depending on how large you want them.

3 Preheat the oven to 170°C (325°F), Gas mark 3.

4 Arrange the meatballs on a large tray or roasting tin and drizzle with a little oil. Bake in the oven for 20 minutes or until the meatballs are just cooked.

5 While the meatballs are cooking you can begin to make up the sauce. Heat a large saucepan with a little drizzle of oil. Add the onion, garlic and ginger and cook over a gentle heat for 2–3 minutes until they begin to soften. Add the curry paste and cook over a very gentle heat for a further 2–3 minutes to bring out the flavours of the paste.

6 Next add the chopped tomatoes and the coconut milk and bring the mixture to the boil. Put the meatballs on top of the sauce in the pan, then reduce the heat and simmer for 15–20 minutes. Season to taste with salt and pepper.

7 Just before serving, sprinkle with some freshly chopped coriander.

SOY AND HONEY GLAZED BELLY OF PORK WITH SEARED SCALLOPS, SAUTEED CABBAGE AND AN APPLE MASH

This is a perfect dinner party recipe, because pork belly and scallops are two ingredients that people find super impressive. The textures and flavours marry very well and the presentation is great, with a nice variety of colours. Ask your butcher to tie and roll the pork belly for you.

SERVES 8

1 pork belly, about 1.3kg/3lb

1 bunch of fresh herbs

2 large cooking apples, peeled, cored and thinly sliced

50g/2oz/¼ cup light brown sugar

6 large potatoes (I normally use Roosters for mashing)

50g/2oz/½ stick butter

50ml/2fl oz/¼ cup pouring cream

125ml/4fl oz/½ cup soy sauce

3 tbsp runny honey

1 head of green kale or cabbage, thinly sliced

2 tsp sunflower oil

150g/5oz/generous ½ cup smoked bacon lardons

25g/1oz/¼ stick butter

18 medium scallops, corals removed

1 Put the pork belly into a large pan. Cover with water and some fresh herbs and bring to the boil. Continue to boil for 1½ hours until the meat is nice and tender. Remove the meat from the pan and allow to cool. Discard the herbs. It is preferable to leave the meat in the fridge overnight, but if not, then leave it for as long as time allows.

2 Place the apples in a medium saucepan with the sugar and 3 tablespoons of water and simmer gently until the apples have softened. Remove the pan from the heat and mash them roughly with the back of a wooden spoon. Allow to cool.

3 Peel the potatoes and cut into small chunks then cook in a saucepan of boiling water until tender. Drain and return the potatoes to the pan and mash with the butter and cream. Mix in the cooled puréed apple.

4 Preheat the oven to 200°C (400°F), Gas mark 6.

5 Cut the pork belly into slices about 2.5cm/1in thick. Heat an ovenproof heavy-based pan and pan-fry the pork slices until they are browned on each side. Mix the soy sauce and honey together and pour into the pan on top of the pork. Let this

mixture bubble for a moment before transferring to the oven for 5–6 minutes. If you don't have an ovenproof pan then transfer everything to a baking tray before placing in the oven.

6 Meanwhile, blanch the kale or cabbage in a pan of boiling water for 2–3 minutes. Heat a large wok and add the oil. Add the smoked bacon lardons and stir-fry until they are crispy then add the blanched cabbage and stir-fry for a further 3–4 minutes until the cabbage is piping hot.

7 Heat another pan with the butter, add the scallops and cook on either side for 60 seconds until sealed.

8 To serve, arrange the cabbage stir-fry on serving plates with the pork resting on top. Pop some of the apple-scented potatoes on top of the pork and place the scallops onto the potatoes. Drizzle the dish with a little of the remaining sauce from the pork pan. Serve and enjoy!

INDIVIDUAL PORK WELLINGTONS WITH SAVOY CABBAGE AND PORT AND RED WINE JUS

This process of cooking pork is exceptional, as it prevents the meat from drying out. There is a tremendous variety of colour in the finished dish, so it is quite visually impressive. Inside each Wellington is an apple and wild mushroom duxelle, which adds loads of flavour, and the red wine jus that it's served with is rich and full-bodied. I normally keep the diced shallots in the sauce but you can sieve (strain) them out if you prefer.

SERVES 4

Sunflower oil, for cooking

4 x pork fillet (tenderloin) portions, about 150g/5oz each

Salt and freshly ground black pepper

25g/1oz/¼ stick butter

2 garlic cloves, peeled and chopped

2 shallots, peeled and finely diced

½ cooking apple, peeled, cored and diced

175g/6oz/1½ cups wild mushroom selection

2 tbsp pouring cream

1 packet of puff pastry, naturally thawed

Plain (all-purpose) flour, for dusting

110g/4oz/1 cup finely grated Parmesan cheese

Ingredients continued $\longrightarrow$

1 Begin by making the pork Wellington. Heat a large frying pan with a little drizzle of oil. Season the pork fillets then place in the pan and fry quickly over a high heat for 3–4 minutes on all sides until lightly browned. You should ensure that you get a good start on the cooking process now, as pork needs to be well cooked. Remove from the heat and allow to cool.

2 Meanwhile, reheat the pan with the butter and add the garlic, shallots and the apple. Cook over a gentle heat for 4–5 minutes until the mixture has softened. Add the wild mushrooms and cook for a further 3–4 minutes to soften the mushrooms. At this stage adjust the seasoning accordingly and add the cream. Remove from the heat and allow the mixture (or duxelle) to cool for a few minutes.

3 Roll out the puff pastry slightly on a floured work surface (counter). Scatter the grated Parmesan over the pastry and then knead the pastry back together again to incorporate the cheese. Roll out the pastry thinly and cut into four rectangular portions.

4 Prepare an egg wash by mixing the egg together with the milk to create a nice glaze.

Continued $\longrightarrow$

EGG WASH

1 egg

2 tbsp milk

PORT AND RED WINE JUS

½ tbsp butter

4 shallots, peeled and sliced

2 garlic cloves, peeled and chopped

2 fresh thyme sprigs

50g/2oz/¼ cup (solidly packed) dark brown sugar

400ml/14fl oz/1¾ cups red wine

1 tsp tomato purée (tomato paste)

1½ tbsp good-quality port

BUTTERED SAVOY CABBAGE

1 head savoy cabbage

50g/2oz/½ stick butter

110g/4oz/scant ½ cup bacon lardons

5 Divide the duxelle among the portions of puff pastry, placing it in the centre of the pastry. Place the pork on top of the duxelle and brush the egg wash around the outer rim of the remaining pastry. Fold the pastry over the pork and seal the edges then brush thoroughly with the egg wash. If you are feeling very creative, cut out some additional shapes from the pastry trimmings and stick them on the top with egg wash. Brush the shapes with a little more egg wash to give a professional finish.

6 To make the port and red wine jus, melt the butter a large saucepan, add the shallots, garlic and thyme and glaze quickly until they are beginning to soften slightly. Next add the brown sugar and allow this to melt and bubble up around the sides of the pan. This will give a nice sweet flavour to the sauce and will provide a nice accompaniment to the pork. Next lower the heat to quite low and pour in the red wine, tomato purée and port. Bring to a gentle boil and cook for about 15 minutes or until reduced to a syrup-style jus.

7 Preheat the oven to 190°C (375°F), Gas mark 5.

8 For the buttered Savoy cabbage, shred the cabbage into thin strips, removing the core and any outer leaves. Bring a large saucepan of salted water to the boil and add the shredded cabbage. Cook vigorously for 3–4 minutes until it has softened but is still a vivid green colour. Drain and run the cabbage under ice-cold water until it has cooled.

9 Heat a large wok with the butter, add the bacon lardons and quickly fry for 3–4 minutes until they are becoming crisp. Add the refreshed cabbage and toss around with the bacon and the melted butter for 3–4 minutes until it has thoroughly heated. Taste and adjust the seasoning accordingly.

10 Place the pork Wellingtons in the oven for 20–25 minutes until the pastry is golden brown.

11 To serve divide the buttered cabbage among serving plates, place the pork Wellingtons on top and pour over the port and red wine jus.

PORK CUTLETS
WITH STICKY GINGER MARINADE

A very simple way to liven up a boring pork chop! The sticky marinade is also particularly nice with pan-fried or grilled salmon.

SERVES 4

4 pork chops

MARINADE

2 tbsp sunflower oil

5 tbsp soy sauce

1½ tbsp runny honey

1 stick lemongrass, finely chopped

2.5cm/1in piece fresh root ginger (gingerroot), peeled and chopped

½ tsp crushed dried chilli flakes

2 garlic cloves, peeled and crushed

½ tsp sesame seeds

1 Place the pork chops in a large shallow non-metallic dish. Stir together all the ingredients for the marinade and pour over the pork chops. Cover and allow to marinate in the fridge for up to 3 hours.

2 Preheat the barbecue (grill) or grill (broiler) and cook the chops on both sides for 3–4 minutes. Allow them to rest on a cooler part of the barbecue until the meat is fully cooked through, about 10 minutes.

3 I like this pork dish served with plain boiled rice or it is nice to slice the pork and serve on top of a salad platter as a warm pork salad.

CHAPTER 4
DESSERTS

You should always leave room for dessert! Although I'm not personally much of a dessert man, I do like to partake on a special occasion. When I was growing up, we always had a dessert on a Sunday, like most families at the time. It was usually some type of baked or steamed pudding. By the end of the meal, the bowl would be licked clean!!

This chapter gathers together my favoured and preferred dessert recipes that I've encountered down the years. A lot of them are real classics that everyone should try.

DEEP-FILLED APPLE AND BLACKBERRY PIE

I always think of this as a real 'Mammy' dish. My mum was a wonderful cook and she often baked deep-filled fruit pies; they always went down a treat with the entire family. Feel free to substitute the blackberries for other fresh or dried fruit.

SERVES 8–10 (V)

350g/12oz/2⅓ cups plain (all-purpose) flour, plus extra for dusting

A pinch of salt

175g/6oz/1½ sticks hard butter, cut into pieces

1 tbsp caster (superfine) sugar

Whipped cream, to serve

FILLING

4–5 cooking apples, peeled, cored and sliced

50g/2oz/⅓ cup blackberries

75g/3oz/generous ⅓ cup caster (superfine) sugar, plus extra for sprinkling

¼ tsp ground cinnamon

GLAZE

1 large egg

100ml/3½ fl oz/scant ½ cup milk

EQUIPMENT

A 23–25cm/9–10in quiche dish or a large pie dish

1 Begin by making the shortcrust pastry. Sift the flour and salt into a large mixing bowl. Add the butter and, using your fingertips, rub the butter into the flour until the mixture resembles fine breadcrumbs. Add the sugar then gradually mix in enough ice cold water (about 6–8 tablespoons) until the mixture comes together into a ball. Knead lightly until the dough is smooth then wrap in clingfilm (plastic wrap) and chill in the fridge for at least 1 hour but for longer if time permits.

2 Preheat the oven to 160°C (325°F), Gas mark 3.

3 Roll out two-thirds of the pastry on a lightly floured surface (counter) and use to line the quiche dish or a large pie dish.

4 To make the filling, mix the sliced apples, blackberries, sugar and cinnamon together in a large mixing bowl. Pour the filling into the centre of the pie then roll out the remaining pastry and use to cover the filling.

5 For the glaze, mix the egg and milk together in a bowl. If you have some scraps of pastry left over then roll them out into thin pieces, cut out some leaves and stick on top of the pie with a little glaze. Brush the top of the pie with the glaze.

6 Bake the pie in the oven for 40–45 minutes or until the pastry is golden brown and well cooked through to the centre.

7 Sprinkle with caster sugar and serve with whipped cream.

POACHED PEARS
WITH CHOCOLATE SAUCE

Readers are always asking me for recipes involving pears. It is actually quite difficult to buy a nice ripe pear these days, so it is good to have a few options for cooking them, which makes unripe ones more edible! This is my twist on a very well tried-and-tested classic French dessert. I like to think that the fruity element in the dish writes off the naughtiness of the chocolate!

SERVES 6 (V)

6 large firm pears
½ lemon, cut into wedges
½ orange, cut into wedges
200g/7oz/scant I cup caster (superfine) sugar
I large glass white wine
Ice cream, to serve

CHOCOLATE SAUCE

250ml/9fl oz/I cup pouring cream
110g/4oz/4 squares dark chocolate (at least 70% cocoa solids)

1 Peel the pears, leaving the stalks intact and remove the cores. Cut a little piece off the base of each pear and stand them upright in a saucepan that fits them comfortably. Add the lemon, orange, sugar and wine and 600ml/I pint/2½ cups water if the pears are not completely covered in liquid and bring to a simmer. Cook for 40–45 minutes until the pears are completely tender.

2 Remove the pan from the heat and allow the pears to cool in the liquid for at least 2 hours, or preferably until the next day to allow the flavours to infuse.

3 To make the chocolate sauce, pour the cream into a saucepan and bring to a gentle boil. Add the boiled cream to the chocolate in a heatproof bowl and stir until smooth.

4 To serve, fan out the pears, leaving the stalks intact and arrange on serving plates. Drizzle a little of the chocolate sauce over each one and serve the remainder separately in a small jug (pitcher). Alternatively, you can just halve the pears and arrange in a serving dish drizzled with the dark chocolate sauce. Serve with oodles of ice cream.

BAKED WHITE CHOCOLATE AND RASPBERRY CHEESECAKE

Raspberries and white chocolate go together beautifully, but be warned: this is a very rich dessert! We are more familiar with non-cook set cheesecakes in this part of the world, but the baked alternative is equally delicious.

SERVES 10–12 (V)

350g/12oz biscuits (cookies), such as ginger nuts (gingersnaps), oreos or chocolate chip cookies

75g/3oz/¾ stick butter, melted

300g/11oz/10 squares white chocolate, broken into pieces

500g/1lb 2oz/2¼ cups cream cheese

300ml/10fl oz/1¼ cups half-fat crème fraîche

250g/9oz/1¼ cups caster (superfine) sugar

2 tsp cornflour (cornstarch)

4 large eggs

½ tsp vanilla extract

110g/4oz/generous ¾ cup fresh or frozen raspberries

TO SERVE

75g/3oz/3 squares white chocolate, melted

Fresh raspberries

EQUIPMENT

A 23cm/9in springform tin (pan)

1 Preheat the oven to 120°C (250°F), Gas mark ½. Line the base of the springform tin with parchment paper.

2 Break the biscuits into fine crumbs and mix in the melted butter. Press the biscuits into the base of the prepared tin in an even layer and chill in the fridge until required.

3 Break the white chocolate into a heatproof bowl then set over a saucepan of gently simmering water and leave until melted. Remove the bowl from the heat and stir until smooth.

4 Place the cream cheese and crème fraîche in a freestanding electric food mixer and beat together until smooth. Add the sugar and cornflour and beat until smooth, then add the melted chocolate.

5 Beat the eggs and vanilla extract together in a bowl then add them to the mixture and beat until the mixture is smooth. Fold in the raspberries at this stage.

6 Pour the mixture evenly on top of the biscuit base and level with a gentle shake. Bake in the oven for about 60 minutes or a little longer if required. The cheesecake may still be a little wobbly, but don't panic!

7 Allow to cool for about 1 hour then transfer to the fridge and chill for 3–4 hours, preferably overnight.

8 Remove the cheesecake from the tin and serve with a drizzle of melted white chocolate and some fresh raspberries.

DARK CHOCOLATE
AND HAZELNUT BROWNIES

They say that chocolate is a natural stimulant. On tasting these brownies, you will definitely agree. Body and soul will both feel better after eating them!

SERVES 8-10 (V)

225g/8oz/8 squares dark chocolate (at least 70% cocoa solids)

225g/8oz/2 sticks butter, chopped into pieces, plus extra for greasing

4 large eggs

225g/8oz/1¼ cups (solidly packed) demerara (raw brown) sugar

100g/3½oz/⅔ cup self-raising (self-rising) flour

75g/3oz/½ cup roughly chopped hazelnuts

110g/4oz/4 squares white chocolate, chopped into pieces

110g/4oz/4 squares plain chocolate, chopped into pieces

Icing (confectioner's) sugar, for dusting

TO SERVE

Ice cream

Chocolate Sauce (see page 143)

EQUIPMENT

A 23cm/9in square cake tin (pan)

1 Preheat the oven to 180°C (350°F), Gas mark 4. Grease and line the base and sides of the cake tin.

2 Melt the dark chocolate and butter together in a heatproof bowl set over a saucepan of simmering water.

3 Beat the eggs and sugar together in a large mixing bowl until light and fluffy. Fold in the melted chocolate and mix well.

4 Sift the self-raising flour and gently fold it into the chocolate and egg mixture with a large metal spoon, then fold in the hazelnuts and chopped chocolate and mix well. Do not overmix, as the air will be knocked out of the mixture.

5 Pour the mixture into the prepared cake tin and bake in the oven for 35–40 minutes or until the centre of the cake feels firm on the top but with an element of softness underneath.

6 Allow the cake to cool slightly in the tin and then after a few minutes remove from the tin and cut into even-sized squares. Dust generously with icing sugar and serve with ice cream and chocolate sauce.

GOOSEBERRY FOOL
WITH TOASTED GRANOLA

———————

This is a great dessert (or indeed breakfast option) for those who are health conscious because the recipe uses natural (plain) yoghurt rather than cream. Though do feel free to use freshly whipped cream if you prefer. The dessert is quite light, so ideal at the end of a heavy meal. You can really play around with the granola recipe and add whatever items you wish, such as dates, apricots, sultanas, or citrus zest. Make extra and retain it to eat as a breakfast cereal. It will last in an airtight container for up to 3 weeks.

SERVES 6 (V)

450g/1lb gooseberries

225g/8oz/1 cup caster (superfine) sugar

400ml/14fl oz/1¾ cups thick natural (plain) yoghurt

4 tsp runny honey (optional)

Fresh mint sprigs, to decorate

GRANOLA

225g/8oz/2⅔ cups porridge oats (oatmeal)

110g/4oz/1 cup flaked (slivered) almonds

110g/4oz mixed fruit, such as apricots, prunes and dates

25g/1oz/generous ⅛ cup hazelnuts

50g/2oz/⅓ cup sultanas (golden raisins)

50g/2oz/¼ cup (solidly packed) demerara (raw brown) sugar

4 tsp runny honey

EQUIPMENT

6 large serving glasses

1 Preheat the oven to 180°C (350°F), Gas mark 4.

2 Begin by making the gooseberry compote. Place the gooseberries, caster sugar and 6–8 teaspoons of water in a medium saucepan and bring to the boil. Reduce the heat and simmer for 10–15 minutes until they just begin to soften. Do not allow the mixture to become smooth – it's nice to have lumps of fruit. Allow to cool completely.

3 Meanwhile, prepare the granola. Spread the oats, almonds, mixed fruit, hazelnuts and sultanas onto a flat baking sheet. Scatter the demerara sugar over the top then drizzle with the honey and bake in the oven for 15–20 minutes until golden brown and crisp. Remove from the oven and allow the granola to cool completely. Store in an airtight container until required.

4 To assemble the fool, simply mix the cooled gooseberry compote into the yoghurt. Do not mix it in entirely; a marbled effect looks more visually impressive. Sweeten with the honey, if desired.

5 Divide the fool mixture among 6 large serving glasses and sprinkle a thin layer of the toasted granola on the top. Decorate with a sprig of fresh mint.

COFFEE LAYER CAKE

A classic and delicious cake, great topped with crushed walnuts.

SERVES 8-10 (V)

225g/8oz/2 sticks butter, softened, plus extra for greasing

225g/8oz/1 cup caster (superfine) sugar

4 large eggs, lightly beaten

225g/8oz/1½ cups plain (all-purpose) flour, sifted

1 tbsp coffee essence

COFFEE ICING (FROSTING)

225g/8oz/generous 2 cups icing (confectioner's) sugar

110g/4oz/1 stick butter, softened

1 tbsp coffee essence

TO SERVE

Apricot jam (optional)

Dark or milk melted chocolate or crushed walnuts

EQUIPMENT

A 23cm/9in loose-bottomed springform tin (pan) or two 20cm/8in sandwich tins

1 Preheat the oven to 180°C (350°F), Gas mark 4. Grease and line the base of the cheesecake tin or sandwich tins.

2 Cream the butter and sugar together in a large mixing bowl until very light and fluffy. Gradually add the eggs and mix in the flour. Pour in the coffee essence and mix well.

3 Pour the mixture into the prepared tin(s) and bake in the oven for 35–40 minutes or until the cake is well set and a skewer inserted into the centre comes away spotlessly clean and dry. If you are using the sandwich tins, 20 minutes should be enough time in which to cook the cakes.

4 Remove the cake(s) from the oven and leave in the tin(s) to cool slightly then remove and allow to cool on a wire rack. Ideally you should have the cake made the day before you need it.

5 To make the icing, cream the icing sugar and butter together in a large mixing bowl for at least 4–5 minutes. Mix in the coffee essence and 1 tablespoon of boiling water. The addition of the boiling water will make the icing really soft.

6 If you have used the springform tin, cut the cake in half horizontally. Spread some creamy butter icing in the middle of the coffee sponge. I normally put a little apricot jam under the top half and put the apricot-coated sponge on top of the butter icing. Spread the remaining butter icing over the top of the cake and drizzle with melted chocolate or sprinkle with crushed walnuts.

KEVIN'S ETON MESS

This is a traditional dessert of crushed meringue, strawberries and cream, which is served at Eton College after their annual cricket match with Winchester College. There are many variations on this dessert, each one delicious, here is mine!

SERVES 6 (V)

300ml/10fl oz/1¼ cups whipping cream

½ vanilla pod (bean)

400g/14oz meringues

225g/8oz/1½ cups fresh strawberries, hulled

Fresh mint sprigs, to decorate (optional)

1 Lightly whip the cream. Cut the vanilla pod in half lengthways and scrape out the seeds with a knife. Add the seeds to the whipped cream.

2 Place the meringues in a separate bowl and smash with a wooden spoon or rolling pin until crushed. Slice the strawberries into rough chunks.

3 There are two main ways that you can present the dessert. Place the crushed meringues in a large mixing bowl, add the strawberries and the vanilla cream mixture and mix everything together. Pile the mixture either into individual serving glasses or a large serving bowl. Alternatively, you could prepare the three elements of the dish (cream, meringue and strawberries) and neatly layer them up in a serving bowl or glasses and decorate with a sprig of mint.

TIP

If you wish, you could drizzle some strawberry coulis over the top to make a 'wetter' dish.

CREPES SUZETTE
WITH STRAWBERRIES AND CREAM

I remember being on a family holiday as a young child and being so very thrilled to be presented with this dish on my first visit to a 'posh' restaurant!

SERVES 4–6 (V)

150g/5oz/1 cup plain (all-purpose) flour

3 large eggs

2 tbsp sunflower oil

Finely grated zest of 1 orange

50g/2oz/¼ cup caster (superfine) sugar

300ml/10fl oz/1¼ cups milk

50g/2oz/½ stick butter, melted, plus extra for cooking

ORANGE SAUCE

110g/4oz/1 stick butter

110g/4oz/generous ½ cup caster (superfine) sugar

4 tbsp Grand Marnier or Cointreau liqueur

Finely grated zest and juice of 2 oranges

2 tbsp brandy (optional)

TO SERVE

Fresh strawberries

Vanilla cream (see tip below)

Brown sugar, for sprinkling

1 Sift the flour into a bowl and make a well in the centre. Add the eggs, oil, melted butter, orange zest, sugar and milk and whisk well until smooth. Allow the batter to rest in the fridge for at least an hour before making the crêpes, to allow the mixture to settle.

2 To cook the crêpes, heat some butter in a crêpe pan or frying pan. Ladle a little batter into the centre, tilting the pan so that the batter covers the surface thinly and evenly and cook on both sides until lightly browned. Slide it out of the pan onto a warm plate and keep warm while you make the rest.

3 To make the sauce, put the butter in a small pan, add the sugar and whisk rapidly over a low heat. Add the Grand Marnier or Cointreau and the orange zest and juice. Bring to the boil, stirring continuously, then cook briskly until the sauce thickens.

4 Pour the sauce into a frying pan over a low heat. Place the crêpes in the sauce one at a time, folding them once, and then again, to make little triangles. Spoon the sauce over the crêpes to make sure they are all soaked with the sauce.

5 If desired, take the frying pan to the table, add a little brandy at the table and very carefully ignite. Serve with a big bowl of strawberries with vanilla cream and brown sugar for sprinkling over the top.

TIP

To make vanilla cream, lightly whip some cream. Cut a vanilla pod in half lengthways then scrape out the seeds with a knife and add the seeds to the whipped cream.

ROCKY ROAD SQUARES

Emily, Sophie and Tom absolutely love these, and no birthday party in the Dundon household is complete without them.

SERVES 8–10

110g/4oz/1 stick unsalted butter, softened

300g/11oz/10 squares dark chocolate (at least 70% cocoa solids), broken into chunks

3 tbsp golden (corn) syrup

200g/7oz Rich Tea or digestive biscuits, crushed to small pieces

75g/3oz/generous ½ cup whole almonds

100g/3½oz marshmallows

110g/4oz/generous ½ cup glacé (candied) cherries, halved

Icing (confectioner's) sugar, for dusting

EQUIPMENT

A 23cm/9in square cake tin (pan)

1 Line the cake tin with a triple layer of clingfilm (plastic wrap) or parchment paper.

2 Combine the butter, chocolate and golden syrup in a saucepan and heat gently, stirring continuously until melted and smooth.

3 Mix the biscuits, almonds, marshmallows and halved cherries together in a large mixing bowl. When the chocolate mixture has melted, pour it onto the biscuit mixture and mix well until combined.

4 Pour the chocolate and biscuit mixture into the prepared cake tin and level with a spatula or mixing spoon. Transfer to the fridge and allow to chill for 3–4 hours or until set.

5 When ready to serve, cut into squares and dust with icing sugar.

CHRISTMAS ICE CREAM LOG

This dessert is an unusual and tasty option for the festive season. The beauty of it is that you can make the log well in advance of Christmas and just keep it frozen until required.

MAKES ABOUT 900ML/1½ PINTS/ 3½ CUPS (V)

150g/5oz/¾ cup caster (superfine) sugar

600ml/1 pint/2½ cups pouring cream

5 egg yolks

1 vanilla pod (bean), split lengthways and seeds scraped out or 1 tsp vanilla extract

Chocolate Sauce (see page 143), to serve

ADDITIONAL FLAVOURINGS

75g/3oz/½ cup sultanas (golden raisins)

110g/4oz/generous ¾ cup glacé (candied) red cherries

50g/2oz/⅓ cup chopped mixed nuts

Finely grated zest of 1 lemon

EQUIPMENT

A 900g/2lb terrine mould or loaf tin (pan)

1 Line the mould or loaf tin with clingfilm (plastic wrap).

2 Place the sugar in a heavy-based pan with 125ml/4fl oz/½ cup water and heat gently over a low heat until the mixture has dissolved. Bring to the boil and boil rapidly for a few minutes until the syrup begins to reach soft-ball stage. Test by quickly dipping the back of two spoons into the syrup – if it strings between them, then it is ready. Alternatively, use a sugar thermometer, if it reads 115°C (239°F) on the thermometer it is ready.

3 Place the cream in a large bowl and whip until soft peaks form. Whisk the egg yolks, vanilla and 2 tablespoons of hand-hot water in a separate bowl until pale and thickened and the whisk leaves a trail in the mixture. Slowly pour in the sugar syrup then fold the mixture into the whipped cream.

4 Place the vanilla mixture into an ice-cream maker and churn for 20–30 minutes until thickened and increased in volume. Don't leave it churning until completely frozen and set, or it will be over-churned and slightly grainy in texture. Mix in the flavourings.

5 When the ice cream is almost set, pour it into the prepared terrine mould or loaf tin, cover with clingfilm and freeze overnight.

6 To serve, remove the ice cream from the freezer and allow to stand for 10 minutes before removing from the tin. Slice into thick wedges and serve with lots of hot chocolate sauce.

APPLE AND CINNAMON CAKE

This is a deliciously moist cake and is extremely versatile. It is a great lunchbox filler or something to take to work for morning coffee. If you warm the cake very gently before serving, it brings out the flavour of the spices. The cake can be made in a 900g/2lb loaf tin (pan) or the mixture can be divided between two 18cm/7in sandwich tins (pans) – cook for about 35 minutes – and sandwiched together with some mascarpone icing.

SERVES 6–8 (V)
Butter, for greasing
250g/9oz/1⅔ cups plain (all-purpose) flour
2 tsp baking powder
2 tsp ground cinnamon
150g/5oz/generous ¾ cup chopped dates
75g/3oz/generous ⅓ cup (solidly packed) dark brown sugar
2 eating apples, peeled and grated
4 tsp chopped walnuts
2 large eggs
100ml/3½fl oz/scant ½ cup orange juice
75ml/3fl oz/⅓ cup sunflower oil

ICING
75g/3oz/generous ⅓ cup mascarpone cheese
2 tsp icing (confectioner's) sugar
Finely grated zest of 1 orange

EQUIPMENT
A 900g/2lb loaf tin (pan)

1 Preheat the oven to 180°C (350°F), Gas mark 4. Grease and line the base of the tin with parchment paper.

2 Sift the flour, baking powder and cinnamon together into a large mixing bowl. Add the chopped dates and make a well in the centre. Next add the sugar, grated apples, walnuts, eggs, orange juice and oil and mix thoroughly until the mixture is well combined.

3 Spoon the mixture into the prepared tin and bake in the oven for 60–70 minutes or until a skewer inserted in the centre comes out clean. Allow the cake to cool in the tin and then invert onto a serving plate.

4 Prepare the icing by beating the mascarpone, icing sugar and grated orange zest together in a large mixing bowl. Spread the icing over the top of the cooled cake and, using a palette knife, create a wavy effect.

BAKED ALASKA

———

Whenever I think of Baked Alaska, I always think of my debutant ball – this was the dessert we ate that night and, all these years on, it still brings a smile to my face when I taste it. As with many retro recipes, it is now making a comeback, and this is a nice raspberry and orange alternative.

SERVES 6 (V)
18cm/7in disc shop-bought plain sponge
4 tbsp Grand Marnier
250ml/9fl oz/1 cup vanilla ice cream
150g/5oz/1 cup raspberries (fresh or frozen)

MERINGUE
175g/6oz/¾ cup caster (superfine) sugar
3 egg whites

RASPBERRY COULIS
200g/7oz/1⅓ cups raspberries
2 tbsp icing (confectioner's) sugar

1 Preheat the oven to 190°C (375°F), Gas mark 5.

2 Begin by making the meringue. Place the sugar and egg whites in a large mixing bowl and beat for 5 minutes until stiff, preferably using a freestanding electric food mixer.

3 Next make the raspberry coulis. Put all the ingredients in a food processor, add 1 tablespoon plus 2 teaspoons of water and whizz to a pulp. Push the mixture through a fine sieve (strainer) set over another bowl, pressing well with the back of a wooden spoon to extract the seeds. Set aside.

4 Place the sponge disc on a large heatproof serving plate and sprinkle with the Grand Marnier until well soaked. Spoon on the vanilla ice cream, then arrange most of the raspberries over the top and around the edge. Using a palette knife, spread enough of the meringue over until everything is completely covered. If you wish, you could use a piping bag (pastry bag) and pipe the meringue mixture all over. It is very important to make sure that there are no holes or gaps in the mixture, as this will cause the ice cream to melt and ooze out unnecessarily.

5 Bake in the oven for about 10 minutes until the meringue is crisp.

6 Spoon the raspberry coulis around the plate and decorate with the remaining raspberries. Serve immediately.

STEAMED MARMALADE PUDDING

Steamed puddings are amongst my favourite desserts. As you already know, I'm a big fan of comfort food and this dessert fits right into the comfort category. If you wish, you can substitute the marmalade for jam (jelly) or lemon curd as a tasty alternative.

SERVES 6–8 (V)

225g/8oz/2 sticks butter, softened, plus extra for greasing

3 tbsp orange marmalade

225g/8oz/1 cup caster (superfine) sugar

Finely grated zest of 2 oranges

5 large eggs, lightly beaten

350g/12oz/2⅓ cups self-raising (self-rising) flour, or plain (all-purpose) flour with 1 tsp baking powder

2 tsp milk (optional)

Softly whipped cream, to serve

EQUIPMENT

A 900g/2lb pudding basin (ovenproof bowl)

1 Lightly grease the pudding basin and place a small parchment disc at the bottom of the basin. Fill a large saucepan with water, about one-third of the way up and bring to the boil.

2 Pour the marmalade into the bottom of the pudding basin.

3 Beat the butter, sugar and grated orange zest together in a large mixing bowl until creamy and fluffy. Add the eggs then sift in the flour and mix thoroughly until completely combined. It is important to scrape down the bowl at this stage to ensure that all of the butter has been incorporated into the pudding mixture. If you find the mixture is a little stiff, you can add the milk to loosen it up.

4 Pour the mixture into the pudding basin. Cover the top with a double thickness of greased and pleated greaseproof paper and foil and secure with string then carefully place the basin in the saucepan. Boil for a couple of moments then reduce the heat to a gentle simmer and simmer for 1½ hours, topping up the water in the pan, if necessary. Remove the pudding from the pan and allow to rest for 5–10 minutes.

5 Invert the pudding onto a serving platter to turn out and remove the parchment paper. Serve with some softly whipped cream.

HONEY ROASTED SPICED FRUITS

This is a simple but attractive dessert which can be served directly from the roasting dish in the middle of the table. Sometimes I make these fruits to give as a gift, piled up in a tin or container, and they are always very well received.

SERVES 6–8 (V)

4 plums, cut into quarters

3 peaches, cut into quarters

3 figs, cut into quarters

2 apples, cut into quarters

2 Conference pears, cut into quarters

110g/4oz/generous ½ cup (solidly packed) soft brown sugar

2 star anise

2 bay leaves

I vanilla pod (bean)

2 tbsp runny honey

250ml/9fl oz/I cup orange juice

Natural (plain) yoghurt or crème fraîche, to serve

I Place all of the fruit in a large bowl and scatter over the brown sugar. Mix in the star anise and bay leaves. Split the vanilla pod in half lengthways and scrape out the seeds with a knife then put both the seeds and the pod into the bowl. Drizzle in the honey and the orange juice and allow to infuse for up to 20 minutes.

2 Preheat the oven to 180°C (350°F), Gas mark 4.

3 Transfer the fruit and all the juices to a large casserole or roasting dish and bake, uncovered, in the oven for 25 minutes.

4 Serve either hot or cold with some yoghurt or crème fraîche.

APPLE AND CRANBERRY FRANGIPANE TART

This is a delicious and sophisticated recipe, which I love to make for a special occasion. You can substitute the cranberries with cranberry sauce.

SERVES 6–8 (V)

150g/5oz/1 cup plain (all-purpose) flour

75g/3oz/generous ⅓ cup caster (superfine) sugar

75g/3oz/¾ stick hard butter, cut into pieces

1 large egg, beaten

Ice cream, cream or custard, to serve

APPLE AND CRANBERRY COMPOTE

3 cooking apples

110g/4oz/½ cup caster (superfine) sugar

4 tsp cranberry juice or water

75g/3oz/¾ cup fresh cranberries

FRANGIPANE

175g/6oz/1½ sticks butter, softened

175g/6oz/¾ cup caster (superfine) sugar

¼ tsp almond extract

3 large eggs, lightly beaten

175g/6oz/1¼ cups ground almonds

25g/1oz/generous ⅛ cup plain (all-purpose) flour

EQUIPMENT

A 20–23cm/8–9in fluted flan ring or loose-bottomed quiche tin or tart tin (pan)

1 Begin by making the pastry. Sift the flour into a large mixing bowl, add the sugar then add the butter and, using your fingertips, rub the butter into the flour until the mixture resembles fine breadcrumbs. Add the beaten egg and mix to bind the mixture together into a ball. Cover the dough in clingfilm (plastic wrap) and allow the pastry to rest in the fridge for a couple of hours.

2 Roll out the pastry on a lightly floured work surface (counter) and use to line the flan ring. Allow to chill until required. Store any leftover pastry in the fridge for up to 7 days.

3 To make the compote, peel, core and chop the apples then place them in a large saucepan with the sugar and cranberry juice or water and heat gently. When the apples are almost soft, mash them a little to break the apple down into smaller pieces. Next add the cranberries and cook for 2–3 minutes. Remove the pan from the heat and allow to cool.

4 To make the frangipane, cream the butter, sugar and almond extract together in a large mixing bowl until light and fluffy. Gradually beat in the eggs, ground almonds and the flour. The mixture should resemble a Victoria sponge consistency. It lasts up to a week in the fridge.

5 Preheat the oven to 180°C (350°F), Gas mark 4.

Continued ⟶

6 Spoon the apple and cranberry mixture into the pastry case then spoon the frangipane on top and spread evenly over to cover the fruit and without mixing the fruit into it. Bake in the oven for 35–40 minutes until the pastry is golden brown, the frangipane is well set and a skewer inserted into the centre comes out clean.

7 Serve the tart warm or cold with ice cream, cream or custard.

VARIATION
Try using blackberries or blueberries.

EVE'S PUDDING

This traditional recipe is an old favourite of mine from my childhood. I love the addition of ground cinnamon, which marries well with the sweet apples and adds an extra flavour to the pudding.

SERVES 6 (V)
110g/4oz/1 stick butter
110g/4oz/generous ½ cup (solidly packed) brown sugar
1 tsp baking powder
225g/8oz/1½ cups plain (all-purpose) flour
A pinch of ground cinnamon
4 large eggs, lightly beaten
Icing (confectioner's) sugar, for dusting
Whipped cream, to serve

APPLE COMPOTE
4 large cooking apples, peeled, cored and sliced
75g/3oz/generous ⅓ cup caster (superfine) sugar
A pinch of ground cinnamon

1 Preheat the oven to 160°C (325°F), Gas mark 3.

2 Begin by making the apple compote. Place the apples in a large saucepan with the sugar and 2 tablespoons of water and cook for 3–4 minutes until they're beginning to turn mushy but not completely stewed. Add the cinnamon and transfer to a casserole or baking dish, about 23cm/9in in diameter. Set aside.

3 To make the pudding, beat the butter and brown sugar together in a large mixing bowl until smooth. Sift the baking powder, flour and cinnamon together. Add the eggs to the butter mixture then add the dry ingredients and mix until everything is well incorporated.

4 Spread the sponge mixture on top of the apple compote in the dish and pop into the oven on the middle shelf for about 35–45 minutes, or until the mixture is set and a skewer inserted in the centre comes out clean.

5 Dust the Eve's pudding with icing sugar and serve with whipped cream.

CHOCOLATE AND HAZELNUT MERINGUE

_____

This lavish meringue cake is a wonderful mountain of delicious ingredients – raspberries, hazelnuts and chocolate. Make sure you fill the meringue at least 4 hours before serving; it will then cut into portions without splintering. When melting the chocolate to make the chocolate curls, there are two main things to remember: melt it slowly and never let it get too hot. The curls can be sprinkled over almost any chocolate dessert for a delicate finishing touch.

SERVES 6–8 (V)

175g/6oz/scant 1¼ cups hazelnuts, skinned and toasted

275g/10oz/2¼ cups icing (confectioner's) sugar, plus extra for dusting

110g/4oz/4 squares dark chocolate, broken into pieces

½ tsp bicarbonate of soda (baking soda)

4 egg whites

A pinch of salt

FILLING

300ml/10fl oz/1¼ cups pouring cream

250g/9oz/1¼ cups mascarpone cheese

225g/8 oz/1½ cups fresh raspberries

CHOCOLATE CURLS

110g/4oz/4 squares dark chocolate (at least 70% cocoa solids), broken into pieces

1 Preheat the oven to 120°C (250°F), Gas mark ½. Line three baking sheets with non-stick parchment paper. Draw a 20cm/8in circle on each piece of paper and then turn the paper over.

2 Place the toasted hazelnuts in a food processor with 3 tablespoons of the icing sugar and process to a fine powder. Add the chocolate and pulse until finely chopped. Set aside.

3 Sift the remaining icing sugar and bicarbonate of soda into a bowl. Whisk the egg whites with the salt in a large bowl until very stiff, but not dry. Whisk in the combined icing sugar and bicarbonate of soda. Carefully fold in the hazelnut and chocolate mixture until well combined. This is best done in a food mixer to make sure everything is mixed in well.

4 Divide the meringue mixture among the 3 circles, spreading into rounds of an even thickness using a spatula. Bake for 5 minutes, then reduce the oven temperature to 110°C (225°F), Gas mark ¼ and bake for a further 1¼ hours until the tops of the meringues are crisp and the insides soft like a marshmallow. Swap the baking sheets during baking to ensure even cooking.

Continued ⟶

5 Slide the meringues, still on the parchment, off the baking sheet onto wire racks and allow to cool for about I hour, or until cold, then peel off the parchment paper.

6 To make the filling, whip the cream in a large mixing bowl until it holds its shape then fold in the mascarpone. Place a meringue on a serving plate. Spread with a third of the cream mixture and raspberries. Place the second meringue on top and press down lightly. Cover with another third of the cream mixture and raspberries. Position the final meringue on top. Chill in the fridge for at least 4 hours, reserving the remaining cream mixture and raspberries for the decoration.

7 For the chocolate curls, place 75g/3oz/3 squares of the chocolate in a heatproof bowl set over a pan of simmering water and heat gently until the chocolate has melted. Remove from the heat and stir in the remaining chocolate. Continue to stir until the chocolate is smooth and glossy. This will help temper the chocolate. Pour the chocolate onto a very cold marble slab and allow to set at room temperature. If you put it in the fridge, the chocolate will lose its wonderful sheen.

8 Holding a large sharp knife at a slight angle, carefully push the blade across the surface of the hardened chocolate to shave off long curls. Always push the blade away from you. You should end up with about 12 chocolate curls.

9 To serve, spoon the remaining cream mixture over the layered meringue and arrange the rest of the raspberries with the chocolate curls on top. Dust lightly with icing sugar and bring straight to the table. Cut into slices and serve.

FROZEN BERRIES
WITH WHITE CHOCOLATE SAUCE

In recent years, I have noticed a real shift back towards simple recipes. This is one such recipe: a super dinner party dessert that can literally be made up whilst someone else is clearing the table. Catherine and I occasionally indulge in these berries as a midnight treat.

SERVES 6 (V)

250g/9oz mixed frozen
  berries

**WHITE CHOCOLATE
SAUCE**

250ml/9fl oz/1 cup pouring
  cream

2 tbsp Baileys

110g/4oz/4 squares good-
  quality white chocolate

Fresh mint sprigs, to
  decorate

EQUIPMENT

4 large champagne flutes or
  other glasses or demi-
  tasse cups

1 Divide the berries among the champagne flutes.

2 Place the cream and the baileys into a large saucepan and bring to the boil.

3 Put the white chocolate into a large heatproof bowl. Pour the boiled cream mixture onto the chocolate and whisk thoroughly until well combined.

4 Pour the sauce on top of the frozen berries then decorate with a sprig of mint and serve immediately.

LEMON AND BLUEBERRY BREAD AND BUTTER PUDDING

The fruit I've chosen to put in this pudding is an unusual but fantastic variation on the traditional version. The beauty of the recipe is that you can indeed vary the fruit as much as you like. For example, sometimes I like to use a mixture of summer fruit together with approximately 75g/3oz/3 squares of white chocolate. The dessert is great served with some extra custard, so if you wish to do this, consider making more than the recipe suggests.

SERVES 6 (V)

75g/3oz/¾ stick butter, at
   room temperature
12 slices of white bread
150g/5oz/1 cup blueberries
Extra custard, to serve

CUSTARD

300ml/10fl oz/1¼ cups
   pouring cream
300ml/10fl oz/1¼ cups milk
4 large egg yolks
Finely grated zest of 1 lemon
75g/3oz/generous ⅓ cup
   caster (superfine) sugar

EQUIPMENT

A 23–25cm/9–10in ovenproof
   dish

1 Generously grease the ovenproof dish with a little of the butter. Remove the crusts from the bread and, using the remaining butter, butter both sides of each slice and then cut each slice into quarters on the diagonals.

2 Arrange a single layer of the bread triangles, slightly overlapping in the bottom of the prepared dish. Scatter over some of the blueberries and place another layer of the bread triangles on top (keeping some for a final layer) and scatter over the remaining berries. Press down gently with a spatula.

3 To make the custard, heat the cream and milk in a saucepan until it almost comes to the boil. Remove the pan from the heat. Meanwhile, whisk the egg yolks, lemon zest and sugar together in a large heatproof bowl set over a pan of simmering water until thickened and the whisk leaves a trail in the mixture. Remove from the heat and beat into the cream mixture until well combined.

4 Pour two-thirds of the custard over the layered-up bread triangles and allow to stand for about 30 minutes or until the bread has soaked up all of the custard.

Continued ⟶

5 Preheat the oven to 180°C (350°F), Gas mark 4.

6 Pour the remaining custard over the soaked bread and butter triangles and arrange the rest of the bread triangles on top. Press down firmly with a spatula so that the custard comes halfway up the bread triangles. Scatter with a few more berries, if you wish, then bake in the oven for 30–35 minutes until the custard is just set and the top is golden brown.

7 To serve, bring the bread and butter pudding straight to the table and have separate jugs (pitchers) of custard to hand around so that everyone can help themselves.

TIP
This is a pudding that can be made in so many different ways. I personally prefer this classic soft-set with its wonderful buttery top. It is also fabulous made with day-old brioche or croissants instead of the traditional white sliced bread.

CHOCOLATE MOUSSE

This is the simplest recipe for chocolate mousse you will ever prepare. There are also many ways to vary the basic recipe. For example, you might wish to use milk or white chocolate instead of (or as well as) dark, although do remember that white chocolate is the most difficult to work with. For more variations, see my tip below.

SERVES 6 (V)

300g/11oz/10 squares dark chocolate (at least 70% cocoa solids), broken into pieces

3 large eggs, separated

225ml/8fl oz/scant 1 cup whipping cream

Fresh fruit, to serve

EQUIPMENT

6 wine glasses or other glasses

1 Melt the chocolate in a heatproof bowl set over a pan of simmering water. Remove from the heat and allow to cool a little.

2 Using a whisk, lightly beat the egg yolks in a mixing bowl then whisk into the melted chocolate until well combined. The mixture will stiffen immediately at this stage, but don't panic.

3 Whip the cream in a separate bowl until soft peaks form then whisk the cream into the chocolate mixture. The cream will soften the mixture down and loosen its consistency.

4 In a clean bowl, whisk the egg whites until very stiff then gently fold them into the chocolate cream mixture with a large metal spoon. This will add air and lightness to the mousse.

5 Divide the mousse among some fancy wine glasses and allow to chill in the fridge for at least 1 hour before serving with some fresh fruit.

TIP

• Sometimes I use some whipped cream in between layers of the chocolate mousse to give a tiered effect in the glass.

• You can add other ingredients to this mousse as well if you wish. Try chopped nuts, grated orange zest or various liqueurs.

RHUBARB
AND GINGER CRUMBLE

———————

Rhubarb and ginger are two flavours that really complement each other and, as rhubarb is also a classic crumble filling, this beautiful recipe manages to be both traditional and a little bit different at the same time.

SERVES 6–8 (V)

6–8 sticks rhubarb, diced into chunks

150g/5oz/¾ cup (solidly packed) demerara (raw brown) sugar

Juice of 1 orange

½ tsp ground ginger (optional)

2 tsp grenadine (optional)

Softly whipped cream, to serve

CRUMBLE

200g/7oz/1⅓ cups plain (all-purpose) flour

A pinch of ground ginger

110g/4oz/generous ½ cup (solidly packed) brown sugar

100g/3½ oz/scant 1 stick cold butter

EQUIPMENT

A 23cm/9in square casserole dish

1 Preheat the oven to 180°C (350°F), Gas mark 4.

2 Put the rhubarb and sugar into a medium saucepan with the orange juice. Add the ground ginger, if desired and cook over a low heat until the rhubarb is just beginning to soften but is not completely stewed. If you are using the grenadine, you can add it at this stage. Pour the rhubarb into the casserole dish.

3 To make the crumble, place the flour and ground ginger into a large bowl. Add the sugar and mix well. Slice in the butter and, using your fingertips, rub in the butter until the mixture resembles coarse breadcrumbs.

4 Pour the crumble mixture over the slightly softened rhubarb and spread it out roughly then bake in the oven for 25–30 minutes until bubbling hot.

5 Serve immediately with softly whipped cream.

LEMON CURD SWISS ROLL

Swiss roll (jelly roll) was a staple teatime treat in so many households when I was growing up and ours was no different. My mother wasn't a big fan of jam, so she always made hers with some homemade lemon curd (see page 217). It's another retro recipe that deserves to make a comeback.

SERVES 6–8 (V)

Butter, for greasing

4 large eggs

110g/4oz/generous ½ cup caster (superfine) sugar, plus 50g/2oz/¼ cup caster sugar for dusting

110g/4oz/generous ¾ cup self-raising (self-rising) flour, sifted

4 tbsp Lemon Curd (see page 217)

LEMON DRIZZLE ICING (FROSTING)

3 tbsp icing (confectioner's) sugar

Juice of 1 lemon (approx)

EQUIPMENT

A 33 x 23cm/13 x 9in oblong Swiss roll (jelly roll) tin (pan)

1 Preheat the oven to 180°C (350°F), Gas mark 4. Grease and line the base and sides of the tin with parchment paper.

2 Begin by making the sponge. Beat the eggs and sugar together in a large mixing bowl until light, aerated and the whisk leaves a figure of eight on the surface when the whisk is lifted out. Gently fold in the sifted flour with a metal spoon. Be very gentle so not to knock any of the air out of the sponge, but also ensure that all of the flour is incorporated. Pour the mixture into the prepared tin and bake in the oven for 20 minutes until well-risen and golden brown. Remove the sponge from the oven, take out of the tin and allow to cool on a wire rack.

3 Before the sponge is fully cooled, invert it onto a sheet of parchment paper dusted with the 50g/2oz/¼ cup caster sugar and spread over the lemon curd with a spoon or palette knife. With the help of the parchment paper, carefully roll up the sponge starting from the longest side and place on a serving plate.

4 To make the lemon drizzle icing, mix the icing sugar and lemon juice together in a bowl until smooth. Drizzle the icing over the Swiss roll and cut into slices to serve.

LEMON CAKE
WITH GRIDDLED STRAWBERRIES

This cake is a wonderfully indulgent dessert that is perfect as a teatime treat or a dinner party finale. It is best eaten not long out of the oven, when it has just begun to cool, which is just as well really, since it doesn't tend to hang around for long. You have been warned...! The cake goes very well with griddled strawberries – these are simply cooked on a griddle pan (grill pan), preferably one that is non-stick and very clean. This gives the fruit a slightly bitter, burnt tinge that is then balanced out by the dusting of icing (confectioner's) sugar.

SERVES 6–8 (V)

175g/6oz/1½ sticks, butter, at room temperature, plus extra for greasing

200g/7oz/generous ¾ cup caster (superfine) sugar, plus extra for dusting

3 large eggs, lightly beaten

175g/6oz/scant 1¼ cups self-raising (self-rising) flour

Finely grated zest and juice of 1 lemon

4–6 tbsp milk

450g/1lb large fresh strawberries, hulled

1–2 tbsp icing (confectioner's) sugar to taste, plus extra for dusting

150ml/5fl oz/⅔ cup double (heavy) cream

150g/5oz/⅔ cup Greek strained yoghurt

EQUIPMENT

Two 18cm/7in non-stick sandwich tins (pans)

1 Preheat the oven to 190°C (375°F), Gas mark 5. Grease the sandwich tins and lightly dust with sugar, shaking out the excess.

2 Place the butter in a bowl with 175g/6oz/scant ¾ cup of the sugar and beat with an electric beater or wooden spoon until light and fluffy. Gradually beat in the eggs, adding a little of the flour if the mixture begins to curdle. Sift over the remaining flour and fold in using a large metal spoon or plastic spatula. Gently fold in the lemon zest and enough milk to achieve a soft dropping consistency.

3 Divide the cake mixture (batter) between the prepared tins and level the top, then make a slight dent in the centre with the back of a wooden spoon. Bake in the oven for 25–30 minutes until well-risen, firm to the touch and just beginning to shrink from the sides of the tins.

4 Place the remaining caster (superfine) sugar in a bowl and stir in the lemon juice until dissolved. Turn the cakes out onto a wire rack and sprinkle over the lemon glaze. Set aside to cool completely.

Continued ⟶

5 Heat a griddle pan (grill pan) over a medium heat. Add the strawberries and cook for 30 seconds–I minute on each side until lightly charred. Transfer to a plate and dust with icing sugar.

6 Lightly whip the cream in a large bowl then fold in the yoghurt and enough of the icing sugar to taste. When the cakes have cooled, spread over half of the yoghurt mixture and then top with half of the strawberries. Sandwich the two halves together and spread over the remaining yoghurt mixture.

7 Arrange the rest of the strawberries on top and dust again with icing sugar. Cut the cake into slices and serve. Enjoy!

CHOCOLATE CHIP COOKIES

Chocolate chip cookies are a firm favourite in our house and when I make them they always go down a treat. You can vary this recipe as much as you like: sometimes I add some mixed spice and dried fruit. Cookies are an ideal lunchbox filler.

SERVES 6–12 (V)

175g/6oz/1½ sticks butter, softened, plus extra melted butter for greasing

175g/6oz/1 cup (solidly packed) light brown sugar

½ tsp vanilla extract

3 large eggs, lightly beaten

350g/12oz/2⅓ cups plain (all-purpose) flour

1 heaped tsp baking powder

A pinch of salt

110g/4oz/⅔ cup mixed chocolate chips

110g/4oz/¾ cup mixed nuts, such as pistachios, walnuts, shelled hazelnuts and pine nuts

1 Preheat the oven to 180°C (350°F), Gas mark 4. Brush a large baking tray (cookie sheet) with melted butter.

2 Cream the butter, sugar and vanilla extract together in a large mixing bowl for 4–5 minutes until light and fluffy. Add the eggs and beat for a few minutes.

3 Sift the flour, baking powder and the salt together. Mix the mixed nuts and chocolate chips together in a separate bowl.

4 Add the sifted flour mixture to the butter and egg mixture and beat slowly until the mixture comes together. Add the chocolate chips and mixed nuts and beat until combined.

5 Break the dough into small balls and place them, making sure they are well spaced out, on the prepared baking tray. Bake in the oven for 12–15 minutes. Allow to cool then serve.

TIP

This mixture freezes quite successfully. I tend to roll the dough into long thick coils before freezing as this makes it easier to cut the dough, then allow to thaw a little before rolling into balls.

PEACH MELBA
WITH BISCUITS

The Peach Melba is a classic dessert, invented around 1892 by the French chef Auguste Escoffier at the Savoy Hotel, London, to honour the Australian soprano Dame Nellie Melba (1861–1931). It is a very simple last-minute dessert, but your presentation style can be as elaborate as you like. My twist on the recipe includes some crushed ginger biscuits (gingersnaps), which add a lovely extra flavour to the finished dish.

SERVES 4 (V)

110g/4oz crushed ginger nut biscuits (gingersnaps)

4 ripe peaches, stoned (pitted) and chopped into 2.5cm/1in cubes

4 scoops vanilla ice cream

50g/2oz/½ cup flaked (slivered) almonds

RASPBERRY COULIS

200g/7oz/1⅓ cups raspberries, fresh or frozen and thawed

1 tbsp icing (confectioner's) sugar

Juice of 1 lemon

EQUIPMENT

4 wide glasses (martini glasses are ideal)

1 To make the coulis, place the raspberries in a food processor with the icing sugar and lemon juice and blitz until they are completely smooth. Pass the mixture through a sieve (strainer) to remove the seeds from the purée. Store in the fridge until required.

2 Meanwhile, divide the crushed ginger biscuits among the glasses and add the chopped peaches. Add a scoop of ice cream and then pour some of the chilled raspberry coulis on top. Scatter with some of the flaked almonds and serve immediately.

STRAWBERRY ROMANOFF

This is a possible contender for the simplest recipe in the book, but it is one of my all-time favourites. There are several different versions of the recipe, some incorporating ice cream or soured cream into the fresh cream, but I just love the simple French version, which is what I've given here. It is delicious on its own or makes a fantastic topping for a crisp meringue or Pavlova.

SERVES 6 (V)

450g/1lb fresh strawberries

Finely grated zest and juice of 1 orange

75ml/3½fl oz/⅓ cup orange liqueur (eg. Grand Marnier or Cointreau)

½ vanilla pod (bean)

250ml/9fl oz/1 cup whipping cream

1 Hull and halve the strawberries and place them in a large bowl. Add the orange zest and mix well. Pour in the orange juice and orange liqueur and mix well. Transfer to the fridge and allow to chill for at least 1 hour, but longer if time permits.

2 Meanwhile, split the vanilla pod in half lengthways and scrape out the seeds into a large mixing bowl with the cream then whip the cream until soft peaks form.

3 Serve the strawberries and their orange liquid with some of the softly whipped vanilla cream.

BAKED APPLES

Baked apples are one of my favourite recipes for comfort eating and they bring back lots of childhood memories.

SERVES 6 (V)

110g/4oz/¾ cup mixed dried fruit, such as raisins and sultanas (golden raisins)

50g/2oz/1 cup fresh white breadcrumbs

50g/2oz/¼ cup (solidly packed) demerara (raw brown) sugar

50g/2oz/½ cup chopped almonds

½ tsp ground cinnamon

Finely grated zest of 1 orange

1 tbsp Irish whiskey

6 cooking apples

50g/2oz/½ stick butter, cut into 6 pieces

Custard or vanilla ice cream, to serve

1 Preheat the oven to 180°C (350°F), Gas mark 4. Line a large shallow dish with parchment paper.

2 Mix the dried fruit with the breadcrumbs, brown sugar and chopped almonds in a large mixing bowl. Add the ground cinnamon and orange zest and mix well. Add the Irish whiskey and mix until combined.

3 Remove the cores from the apples and place them in the prepared baking dish. Fill the cavity of each apple with the fruit mixture and place a piece of butter on top. Bake in the oven for about 25 minutes or until they are soft and the filling looks nice and crunchy.

4 Serve immediately with jugs (pitchers) of custard or scoops of vanilla ice cream.

ORANGE DRIZZLE CUPCAKES

These make a perfect treat for any occasion, such as a child's birthday party or even a simple summer barbecue. Vary the flavouring as you wish.

SERVES 12 (V)

200g/7oz/1¾ sticks butter, softened

200g/7oz/1 cup caster (superfine) sugar

Finely grated zest of 1 orange

5 large eggs

400g/14oz/2⅔ cups plain (all-purpose) flour, sifted

1 tsp baking powder

2 tsp milk (optional)

TOPPING

110g/4oz/1 cup icing (confectioner's) sugar

Juice of 1 orange (approx)

EQUIPMENT

12-hole muffin tray

1 Preheat the oven to 180°C (350°F), Gas mark 4. Line a 12-hole muffin tray with deep muffin cases (if you prefer you can use smaller bun tins (pans) or even some mini muffin trays).

2 Beat the butter, sugar and grated orange zest together in a large mixing bowl until the mixture is really light and fluffy. It is important to spend a little time on the creaming stage to make sure that the mixture is very light prior to adding the eggs and flour.

3 Add the eggs, flour and baking powder. If you find the mixture is a little tight you can add the milk to loosen it up a little. Divide the mixture (batter) among the muffin cases, filling them about three-quarters full, and bake in the oven for 20–25 minutes until well-risen and cooked through. Remove from the oven and allow to cool in the muffin tray.

4 To make the topping, mix the icing sugar and orange juice together in a bowl until a dropping consistency has been achieved then drizzle over the top of the cakes in an ad-hoc fashion, allowing the icing to drizzle down the sides of the cupcakes. Alternatively, you can spread the icing over the top of the cakes.

BAILEYS CREME BRULEE TART

This is a very popular recipe in our American restaurants, Raglan Road. It's a Bailey's-flavoured crème brûlée cooked in a pastry case. Decadent and indulgent, this is the perfect dinner party dessert.

SERVES 8 (V)

Butter, for greasing

1 quantity Sweet Pastry (see page 161)

600ml/1 pint/2½ cups pouring cream

2 tbsp Baileys

6 large egg yolks

150g/5 oz/¾ cup caster (superfine) sugar, plus extra for dusting

EQUIPMENT

A 23cm/9in loose bottomed flan ring, quiche tin or tart tin (pan)

1 Grease the flan ring and line with sweet pastry. Blind bake the tart case (see tip below).

2 Lower the oven temperature to 150°C (300°F), Gas mark 2.

3 Put the cream and Baileys into a small saucepan and bring to the boil.

4 Whisk the egg yolks and sugar together in a large heatproof bowl until they are light and creamy then pour in the boiled cream. Whisk until combined. Allow to rest for a few minutes until the froth settles, or skim the froth with a slotted spoon.

5 Pour the mixture into the prepared tart case and bake in the oven for 45–50 minutes until just about set. Remove from the oven and allow to cool. Store in the fridge until required.

6 To serve, dust some caster sugar over the tart and use a chef's blowtorch to lightly glaze the top. Alternatively, place under a hot grill, watching carefully, until the top is browned.

TIP

To blind bake: preheat the oven to 190°C (375°F), Gas mark 5. Line the tart case with a layer of parchment paper and fill with rice/lentils/chickpeas or baking beans (pie weights). Bake the tart in the oven for 15 minutes, then remove the beans and parchment paper and bake for a further 8 minutes. Remove from the oven and brush with beaten egg white then return to the oven for 3–4 minutes to create a crisp crust.

SUMMER BERRY JELLY

Not just a normal jelly, this is a real treat to serve at a special occasion. Sometimes I use pink Prosecco instead of champagne and it works wonderfully.

SERVES 6

3 gelatine leaves

300ml/10fl oz/1¼ cups champagne or good-quality sparkling wine

75g/3oz/generous ⅓ cup caster (superfine) sugar

350g/12oz mixed summer fruits, such as strawberries, raspberries and blueberries

EQUIPMENT

6 tall champagne flutes or other glasses

1 Soak the gelatine leaves in a bowl of cold water for at least 10 minutes until soft. Make sure the leaves are immersed in the water.

2 Pour the champagne into a large saucepan and add the sugar. Heat, but do not boil, and watch carefully at this stage because you need it to be just shy of boiling point.

3 Using a fine sieve (strainer), drain the gelatine leaves and give them a good shake to remove the excess water then add the gelatine to the warmed champagne and whisk until it is all incorporated in the liquid. Allow to stand for 7–8 minutes.

4 Meanwhile, slice the fruits as desired and divide them among the champagne flutes.

5 Pour the champagne mixture on top of the summer fruits and transfer to the fridge to set for at least 4 hours but preferably up to 12 hours or more.

6 Remove from the fridge and serve immediately.

CHAPTER 5

KITCHEN ESSENTIALS

BECHAMEL SAUCE

The mother of all sauces. Béchamel is a white sauce that can be used in so many different ways and is an essential part of dishes such as lasagne. It is a great sauce to have in the freezer.

**MAKES ABOUT 600ML/
1 PINT/2½ CUPS (V)**

600ml/1 pint/2½ cups milk
1 small onion studded with about 8 cloves
50g/2oz/½ stick butter
50g/2oz/⅓ cup plain (all-purpose) flour
½ glass white wine
Salt and freshly ground black pepper

1 Place the milk and studded onion in a saucepan and bring to the boil. Remove the pan from the heat and discard the onion.

2 Melt the butter slowly in another small pan, then add the flour and mix until combined. Cook over a low heat for 2 minutes to take the taste of the flour away. Gradually whisk in the boiling milk and white wine and continue to stir, especially around the edges, until it comes to the boil again. Reduce the heat to low and cook for 10–15 minutes. Season to taste with salt and pepper before serving.

VARIATIONS

You can add the following to the sauce:
• In a separate pan, fry 110g/4oz/¾ cup mushrooms in butter.
• 2 tablespoons of chopped fresh parsley.
• 1 teaspoon of wholegrain mustard and 1 sautéed leek.
• 75g/3oz/¾ cup grated cheese, such as Cheddar, mozzarella or Parmesan

BEARNAISE SAUCE

There are several ways to make this sauce, but the method that follows is the one I find works best. Just be careful not to add too much heat to the bowl, as the eggs have a tendency to scramble. This sauce does require a little effort – but an effort that is well worth it!

SERVES 6 (V)
5 black peppercorns
2 tbsp dry white wine
2 tbsp tarragon vinegar
I small shallot, peeled and
  sliced
I bay leaf
3 large egg yolks
110g/4oz/½ cup clarified
  butter (see tip)
2 tsp chopped fresh tarragon
I tsp chopped fresh chervil

I Place the peppercorns, white wine, vinegar and sliced shallot into a small saucepan with the bay leaf and bring to the boil. Reduce the heat and allow to simmer for about 5 minutes until the volume has reduced to half the original volume.

2 Strain the mixture through a sieve (strainer), reserving the liquid, then pour this reduced liquid into a large spotlessly clean heatproof bowl with the egg yolks. Just like hollandaise sauce (see page 195), set the bowl over a pan of simmering water and whisk vigorously until the mixture has become pale and creamy.

3 Slowly pour in the clarified butter, beating well between each addition until all of the butter has been added. Again you must exercise caution when doing this and also make sure that the bowl is not overheating. Whisk in a little boiling water if required to thin down the sauce. When the butter has been added, remove the sauce from the heat and add the chopped tarragon and chervil.

4 Serve immediately with beef fillet.

TIP
To make clarified butter, melt the butter in a saucepan, then remove from the heat and allow to rest. The clarified butter will rise to the top. Strain off and keep the top liquid; this is the clarified butter. The milky substance at the bottom can be discarded.

HOLLANDAISE SAUCE
AND DERIVATIVES

———————

Hollandaise sauce is a very popular condiment that has survived the test of time. Traditionally it is often served with fish, and it is an integral part of the much-loved Eggs Benedict. Regardless of how many times you have made hollandaise sauce, you must still employ the same level of care and precision: mistakes can easily be made. That being said, don't be deterred from making it; if you follow the method carefully it will work out perfectly.

SERVES 6 (V)
150g/5oz/1¼ sticks butter
3 large egg yolks
1 tsp white wine vinegar or lemon juice
Ground white pepper

1 Heat a large saucepan of water and keep it on a very gentle simmer.

2 Melt the butter in another pan and as soon as it has melted remove from the heat – keep it warm but not bubbling (lukewarm is fine).

3 Place the egg yolks in a large spotlessly clean heatproof (either glass or stainless steel) bowl with the wine vinegar or lemon juice and set the bowl over the pan of simmering water. Continue to whisk at all times until the egg yolks become light and creamy in both colour and consistency. You need to be very careful at this stage because the line between creamy and scrambled is indeed very fine!

4 Pour in the melted butter very slowly while continuing to whisk at all times. It's a bit of a balancing act at this stage because you will need to take the bowl on and off the saucepan while whisking in the butter but do persevere – the end result is worth it all. If, after adding all the butter, the sauce is still a little thick for your liking, whisk in 4 teaspoons of boiling water. Season to taste with white pepper.

Continued ⟶

5 If you want to store the sauce for up to I hour I find it best to put it in a china teapot kept near the cooker.

DERIVATIVES

Sauce Bavaroise:	Hollandaise with added cream, horseradish and thyme.
Sauce Crème Fleurette:	Hollandaise with crème fraîche added.
Sauce Dijon:	Hollandaise with Dijon mustard.
Sauce Maltaise:	Hollandaise to which blanched orange zest and the juice of a blood orange is added.
Sauce Mousseline/Chantilly:	Produced by folding whipped cream into hollandaise.
Sauce Noisette:	Made with browned butter (beurre noisette).

BEURRE BLANC

This is a great recipe to have in your culinary repertoire, as it is a last-minute sauce that goes wonderfully with lots of different things, particularly fish or chicken. Serve it sparingly, though, as it is not the healthiest option!

SERVES 6 (V)

100ml/3½fl oz/scant ½ cup white wine

Juice of ½ lemon

2 small shallots, peeled and finely diced

110g/4oz/1 stick cold butter, cubed

Salt and freshly ground black pepper

1 tbsp snipped fresh herbs (optional)

1 Place the wine and lemon juice into a medium shallow saucepan with the diced shallots and bring to the boil. Continue to boil until reduced by about a half.

2 Strain the liquid through a fine sieve (strainer) into a clean pan to remove the shallots. Reheat the mixture if it has cooled down a little.

3 Next, using a whisk, whisk in the butter, piece by piece, whisking well between each addition until all of the butter has been incorporated into the sauce. I find the best way to do this is to whisk in the butter while taking the pan on and off the heat as this will prevent the sauce from splitting. Season lightly with a little salt and pepper and, if desired, you can add some snipped fresh herbs.

APPLE SAUCE

There are certain well-established food pairings and I think apple with pork is perhaps one of the best known. Sharp fruits always go so well with savoury items – be it cranberry with turkey, apple with pork or pineapple with bacon. This recipe makes a lovely sweet compote that can also be served with dessert recipes, such as pancakes.

MAKES ABOUT 2 SMALL JARS (V)

6 eating apples (Granny Smith work well), peeled, cored and quartered

75g/3oz/generous ⅓ cup caster (superfine) sugar

½ vanilla pod (bean)

Juice of ½ lemon

1 Place the apples in a large saucepan with the sugar. Scrape the seeds out of the vanilla pod and add them and the pod to the pan. Add the lemon juice and 50ml/2fl oz/¼ cup water and bring to the boil. Boil for about 10–12 minutes until the mixture is thick and pulpy.

2 Remove the vanilla pod and transfer the sauce to sterilised jars. Store until required. You could store this in the fridge for up to 7 days.

MINT SAUCE

Mint sauce is the classic condiment to serve with roast lamb. There are all sorts of variations on the recipe, but I like to keep mine nice and simple.

MAKES 1 SMALL JAR (V)

110g/4oz fresh mint, chopped

2 tbsp caster (superfine) sugar

50ml/2fl oz/¼ cup white wine vinegar

Juice of ½ lemon

1 Place 1 tablespoon of fresh mint, the sugar, vinegar and 1 tablespoon of water into a saucepan and bring to a gentle boil. Boil for a few minutes until the mixture has reduced by about a half.

2 Meanwhile, place the remaining chopped mint in a large heatproof bowl with the lemon juice. Pour the hot vinegar and sugar mixture onto the chopped mint mixture. Cover and allow to stand for a few hours then store in the fridge until required. It can be kept in the fridge for up to 2 weeks.

THE PERFECT GRAVY

Gravy is an old family favourite and can make or break a good dinner. There are lots of different ways of making gravy, but the best (and possibly easiest) way is to use the fat from a roast joint of meat.

SERVES 6

1 heaped tbsp plain (all-purpose) flour

150ml/5fl oz/⅔ cup red wine

600ml/1 pint/2½ cups good-quality chicken or beef stock (see pages 202–3)

2 tsp redcurrant jelly

2 fresh thyme sprigs, chopped

Cracked black pepper

1 When you have cooked your joint of meat, remove the meat from the roasting tray and allow to rest.

2 Depending on what you have cooked, if there is lots of excess fat you will need to remove some of it.

3 Now put the roasting tray on the hob over a medium heat and heat until the fat bubbles up. Sprinkle in the flour and stir until the flour has absorbed all the liquid. Don't worry about any lumps that form at this stage. Mix well.

4 Next pour in the red wine and whisk well, trying to mix the wine into the thickened fat. Gradually whisk in the stock, making sure that you have incorporated all of the flour mixture. Sieve (strain) the mixture into a clean saucepan and add the redcurrant jelly and chopped thyme. Bring the mixture to the boil and season accordingly with a little cracked black pepper.

5 Serve as required.

VARIATIONS

Other items can be added to the gravy as well if you so desire:
- Few tablespoons of cooked bacon lardons
- Few tablespoons of diced chorizo
- Few tablespoons of diced shallots and tomatoes
- Few tablespoons of wholegrain mustard
- 2–3 tablespoons pouring cream
- Few tablespoons of chopped mixed herbs

PORT AND CRANBERRY RELISH

For me, Christmas is not complete without this relish. I also like to make it throughout the year to serve with cold meat and cheese.

MAKES 1 x 450G/1LB JAR (V)

225g/8oz/2 cups fresh cranberries

1 small cooking apple, peeled, cored and diced

75g/3oz/generous ⅓ cup (solidly packed) light brown sugar

50ml/2fl oz/¼ cup port

1 cinnamon stick

Finely grated zest of 1 orange

1 Put the cranberries and apple into a medium saucepan with the sugar and port and bring to a gentle boil. Add the cinnamon stick and grated orange zest and continue to boil rapidly for about 10 minutes until the mixture is thick and pulpy.

2 Remove the cinnamon stick and transfer the relish to a sterilised jar. Store until required. It will last 3 months.

KEVIN'S TARTARE SAUCE

The perfect accompaniment to fish, this recipe is infinitely superior to a jar of ready-made!

MAKES ABOUT 250G/9OZ/1 CUP (V)

250g/9oz/1 cup mayonnaise

2 tbsp chopped gherkins

1 tbsp capers

2 shallots, peeled and finely diced

1 tbsp chopped fresh parsley

½ tsp Dijon mustard

1 Put the mayonnaise into a large mixing bowl, add the chopped gherkins, capers, shallots and parsley into the mixture. Next mix in the Dijon mustard and mix really well.

2 Store in a container or jar in the fridge until required.

BEEF STOCK

There is nothing like well-made beef stock. It is delicious in gravies, soups, sauces and I particularly love it in French onion soup (see page 16).

**MAKES 1.7 LITRES/
3 PINTS/1¾ QUARTS**
1kg/2lb 4oz beef bones
3 large carrots
2 celery sticks
1 onion
2 bay leaves
3 fresh rosemary sprigs
3 fresh parsley sprigs

1 Preheat the oven to 180°C (350°F), Gas mark 4.

2 Place the beef bones in a large roasting tray and cook in the oven for 1 hour or until the bones are well browned.

3 Transfer the bones to a large saucepan, then add the carrots, celery, onion, bay leaves and herbs, cover with water and bring to the boil. Reduce the heat and simmer for a further 2 hours, skimming the surface every so often to get rid of any unnecessary residue.

4 Strain through a fine sieve into a bowl then cover and allow to cool, preferably overnight.

5 The next morning you can just scrape off the fat, which will now have solidified on the top. Store in the fridge for up to 5 days or freeze for up to 3 months.

CHICKEN STOCK

Homemade stock is so simple to make that you really have no excuses for using cubes or store-bought. I normally make mine in bulk and then store it in the freezer until required. Remember that some effort is always better than no effort, so perhaps save the carcass from your Sunday roast chicken. You can freeze roasted chicken carcasses for a little while until you have a collection and then make a large batch of stock.

**MAKES ABOUT
1.7 LITRES/3 PINTS/
1¾ QUARTS**

Chicken bones from 2
   carcasses

1 carrot

1 celery stick

1 onion

2 bay leaves

2 fresh thyme sprigs

2 fresh tarragon sprigs

6–8 black peppercorns

1 x 400g tin (can) chopped
   tomatoes (optional)

Here are two different ways of making fresh stock:

BROWN STOCK

1 Preheat the oven to 190°C (375°F), Gas mark 5.

2 Place the bones and vegetables in a large roasting tray and cook in the oven for about 45 minutes. Remove them from the oven and place in a large saucepan with the herbs, chopped tomatoes and about 2.4 litres/4 pints/4¼ quarts water. Bring to the boil then reduce the heat and simmer for about 2 hours. Remove and discard the bones and vegetables.

3 Keep the liquid and use as required. When it is refrigerated the fat will come to the top and you can just scoop that off. Store in the fridge or freezer.

USES FOR BROWN STOCK

French onion soup, casseroles, gravies, etc.

WHITE STOCK

1 Follow the same method for brown stock but there is no need to roast the bones and no need to add the tomatoes.

USES FOR WHITE STOCK

Soups, velouté, cream-based sauces, etc.

VEGETABLE STOCK CUBE ALTERNATIVE

When I was training as a chef, every single recipe required a 'bouquet garni'. Nowadays, lots of convenient instant stocks are available, but you still can't beat the classic version. This is a very simple way of adding flavour to a soup, broth or casserole.

MAKES 1 (V)
1 carrot
2 celery sticks
½ leek
3 fresh parsley sprigs
2 fresh tarragon sprigs
3 large fresh thyme sprigs

Very simply just tie all the ingredients together with some string and use as required. Sometimes people like to use some muslin (cheesecloth) to wrap around the vegetables and put in some black peppercorns, etc. It is always removed prior to serving.

TIP
If you wish, you can infuse this parcel into a large pot of water and simmer for up to 2 hours and then discard the parcel and retain the reserved cooking liquor as a simple clear vegetable stock.

AROMATIC FISH STOCK

People are often confused about fish stock because convenience fish stock is not readily available. However, a homemade version is so simple to make and it freezes well for use at a later time. Fish stock makes a wonderful addition to chowders or other fish sauces.

**MAKES ABOUT
2 LITRES/3½PINTS/
2 QUARTS**

450g/Ilb skin from fish
I celery stick
3 black peppercorns
I bay leaf
Fresh parsley stalks
I lemon wedge

1 Place all the ingredients in a large saucepan and bring to the boil for 20 minutes.

2 Strain through a fine sieve and keep the liquid. Transfer to suitable containers and use as required. Store in the fridge or freezer.

SUMMER HERB MARINADE

This marinade works very well on sea bass, salmon, turbot, prawns (shrimp) or scallops, and is also wonderful with chicken or lamb. Use a selection or combination of herbs to add a depth of flavour to the dish.

MAKES ENOUGH FOR 6 PORTIONS

4 tbsp chopped mixed fresh herbs, including parsley, coriander (cilantro), lemon thyme, fresh sage, chives, mint, dill and fennel

2 spring onions (scallions), trimmed and chopped

3 garlic cloves, peeled and chopped

1 tbsp capers

Juice and finely grated zest of 1 lime

150ml/5fl oz/⅔ cup sunflower oil

Salt and freshly ground black pepper

1 Mix the chopped herbs, spring onions and garlic together in a large bowl. Add the capers, lime juice and zest and mix well. Pour in the oil, whisking well and then add a little salt and pepper to taste. Use as required.

2 The marinade can be stored overnight in the fridge.

DRY MEAT RUBS
FOR THE BARBECUE

———————

Why not try this selection of meat rubs to add great flavour to your barbecued (grilled) meats?

MAKES ENOUGH FOR 6 PORTIONS

CHILLI MARINADE
(Delicious on chicken, pork or fish)

1 tsp paprika

½ tsp cayenne pepper

2 chopped red chillies

2–3 black peppercorns

2–3 fresh thyme sprigs

2 garlic cloves, peeled and finely chopped

CITRUS MARINADE
(Delicious on chicken or fish)

Finely grated zest of 1 lemon

Finely grated zest of 1 orange

2 tsp rock salt

2 fresh rosemary sprigs

2 garlic cloves, peeled and chopped

CURRIED MARINADE
(Delicious on pork, chicken or lamb)

½ tsp turmeric

½ tsp ground coriander

1 tsp ground cumin

½ tsp ground ginger

½ tsp Chinese five spice

1 tbsp sunflower oil

CHILLI MARINADE

Place all the ingredients in the food processor and blitz until smooth then pour the marinade onto the meat. Cover and allow to marinate in the fridge. If possible, leave the meat in the marinade for up to 12 hours before cooking.

CITRUS MARINADE

Mix all the ingredients together and rub lightly on the top of the meat or fish. Cover and allow to marinate if time allows. Grill or bake as required.

CURRIED MARINADE

Mix all the spices together with the oil and then spread over the meat.

BASIL PESTO

This well-loved versatile paste can be added to cooked pasta or used as a salad dressing. It is also delicious spread onto a thin piece of chicken or fish and grilled. Mixing pesto into mayonnaise or crème fraîche makes a nice change for salads, sandwiches and baguettes.

MAKES ABOUT 250ML/9FL OZ/I CUP

I large handful of fresh basil leaves

4 tsp freshly grated Parmesan cheese

Juice of ½ lemon

2 tsp pine nuts (toasted or untoasted)

100–150ml/3½–5fl oz/scant ½–⅔ cup olive oil

2 garlic cloves, peeled and crushed

I Place all the ingredients in a food processor or blitz with a hand-held electric blender until smooth.

2 The basil pesto will last in the fridge for up to 3 weeks. Although it will darken slightly in colour, it will still be delicious, as the flavours will just be more mature. If you are unsure what you intend to use the pesto for, I would suggest making it a little thicker and adding extra oil as required.

BLACK OLIVE TAPENADE

This is a delicious paste that is simple to make and will add a sense of the Mediterranean to your food.

MAKES ABOUT I JAR

250g/9oz/1½ cups black olives, stoned (pitted)

3 garlic cloves, peeled

150ml/5fl oz/⅔ cup olive oil, plus extra if needed

Juice of ½ lemon

I tbsp chopped walnuts

3–4 tinned (canned) anchovy fillets

I Place all the ingredients in a food processor and blitz for 2–3 minutes until a suitable smooth consistency is achieved. If you would like to alter the consistency you can add a little extra olive oil to the purée.

2 This paste can be stored in the fridge for 7 days. Store it in a sterilised jar or container in the fridge and cover the top of the paste with 4 teaspoons of olive oil.

SERVING SUGGESTIONS

• Pile some of the tapenade on top of cod and bake in an oven preheated to 190°C (375°F), Gas mark 5 for 15–20 minutes to achieve a nice crust.
• Use to spread on toasted bread or ciabatta.
• Mix into cooked pasta with some Mediterranean roasted vegetables.
• Serve as part of an antipasto platter.

WHITE YEAST BREAD

Who doesn't like delicious, soft, homemade bread? The basic dough can also be used as the base for a homemade pizza, or it can be flavoured as desired and moulded into individual bread rolls.

MAKES I LOAF (V)

450g/Ilb/3 cups strong white bread flour, plus extra for dusting

½ tsp salt

25g/Ioz fresh yeast

About 300ml/I0fl oz/I¼ cups hand-hot water (35°C/95°F)

I tbsp olive oil

EGG WASH

I egg

2 tbsp milk

1 Mix the flour and salt together in a large mixing bowl.

2 Dissolve the yeast in the water, then pour in the oil and add to the flour and, using your hands, combine until a dough forms. Turn the dough out onto a floured work surface (counter) and knead for about 7–10 minutes or until elastic. The dough should have all come together and formed a nice smooth ball.

3 Transfer the dough to a large bowl and cover with clingfilm (plastic wrap) or a clean tea towel (dishtowel) and leave in a warm, draught-free place until the dough has doubled in size. This should take just short of I hour.

4 Preheat the oven to 190°C (375°F), Gas mark 5.

5 For the egg wash, mix the egg and milk together and set aside.

6 After the dough has doubled in size, remove the clingfilm and punch it down gently to deflate the risen dough. Again transfer to a lightly floured work surface and knead for a moment or two, then mould into a large round shape and place on a flat baking sheet lined with a disc of parchment paper. Brush with a little egg wash then dust with additional flour and bake in the oven for 40–45 minutes or until firm to the touch.

7 Allow to cool slightly on the tray and then slice as required.

GUINNESS AND PECAN BREAD

This delicious bread is best eaten as soon as it is cool enough to handle. If you want to keep it for any longer, sprinkle a little water over the crust as soon as it comes out of the oven and wrap in a clean tea towel (dishtowel) to prevent the crust from becoming too hard.

MAKES I LOAF

450g/1lb/3 cups wholemeal (wholewheat) flour

110g/4oz/scant ¾ cup plain (all-purpose) flour, plus extra for dusting

1 tsp bicarbonate of soda (baking soda)

1 tsp salt

50g/2oz/⅔ cup rolled oats

50g/2oz/⅓ cup pecan halves, roughly chopped

2 large eggs

150ml/5fl oz/⅔ cup Guinness

225ml/8fl oz/scant 1 cup buttermilk

2 tbsp treacle

Butter, to serve

1 Preheat the oven to 180°C (350°F), Gas mark 4.

2 Put the wholemeal flour into a bowl then sift over the plain flour, bicarbonate of soda and salt. Stir in the rolled oats and pecans.

3 Break the eggs into a jug (pitcher) and beat lightly, then stir in the Guinness, buttermilk and treacle, whisking to combine. Make a well in the centre of the dry ingredients and gradually add enough of the egg mixture to mix to a soft dough.

4 Turn out on to a lightly floured work surface (counter) and knead very lightly, then shape into an oval and place on a lightly floured baking sheet. Cut a deep cross in the top and bake for 15 minutes, then reduce the oven temperature to 170°C (325°F), Gas mark 3 and bake for a further 20–25 minutes or until the loaf sounds hollow when tapped on the bottom. Transfer to a wire rack (cooling rack) to cool.

5 To serve, eat while still warm, cut into slices with lashings of butter.

CHEESY SCONES

This is a really nice alternative to traditional white soda bread. The scones stay fresh for 3–4 days in your bread bin and they also freeze quite successfully. You can adjust the flavour to suit yourself, using different types of cheese, or other flavourings entirely.

MAKES 9–12

Butter, for greasing, plus extra to serve

450g/1lb/3 cups plain (all-purpose) flour, plus extra for dusting

1 tsp bicarbonate of soda (baking soda)

½ tsp salt

175g/6oz cheese, such as Cheddar cheese or mozzarella, grated

350ml/12fl oz/1½ cups buttermilk

1 Preheat the oven to 180°C (350°F), Gas mark 4. Grease a flat baking tray.

2 Sift the flour into a large mixing bowl. Sift in the bicarbonate of soda – it is vitally important that the soda be sifted, as it tends to clump together. Add the salt then add 75g/3oz grated cheese to the dry ingredients and mix well. Pour in the buttermilk and mix until a soft sticky dough has been achieved.

3 Transfer the dough to a well-floured work surface (counter) and knead for a moment or two. Using a sharp knife, cut the dough into 9–12 squares or triangles (or if you wish to use a round scone cutter, you can do). Place the scones on the prepared baking tray and sprinkle the remaining cheese over the top of the scones.

4 Bake for 25–30 minutes until they are golden brown and the cheese is melted through. Serve immediately with lashings of butter.

SAUCE ANGLAISE

Sauce Anglaise is a homemade egg custard. It is a great accompaniment to serve either hot or cold with a wide range of desserts. I particularly recommend it with a traditional steamed pudding (such as Eve's Pudding on page 162).

**MAKES ABOUT 600ML/
1 PINT/2½ CUPS (V)**
½ vanilla pod (bean)
600ml/1 pint/2½ cups milk
6 large egg yolks
75g/3oz/generous ⅓ cup
 caster (superfine) sugar

1 Scrape out the seeds from the vanilla pod and add them to a medium saucepan with the vanilla pod and the milk. Bring the mixture to a gentle boil.

2 Meanwhile, beat the egg yolks and sugar together in a heatproof bowl until they are pale and creamy. Pour the boiled milk onto the egg mixture and whisk well until combined.

3 Return the mixture to a clean saucepan and stir continuously using a wooden spoon until the mixture coats the back of a spoon. Remove the vanilla pod from the mixture at this stage and use as required. This sauce is best served warm, but if desired allow to cool then store in a container in the fridge for up to 3 days and serve cold.

TIP
If you wish to vary the recipe slightly, you can substitute some of the milk for some fresh pouring cream (about 150ml/5fl oz/ ⅔ cup) or even some fruit coulis (see page 181). Continue to cook in the same way.

BERRY COMPOTE

Berry compote is a great thing to have in the fridge for a variety of different uses. It works wonderfully stirred into natural (plain) yoghurt or fresh cream to make a mixed berry fool. It can also add a nice sharp cut to a variety of desserts – anything from a simple bowl of homemade vanilla ice cream to a decadent chocolate tart.

MAKES 250G/9OZ (V)

250g/9oz mixed fresh or frozen berries such as strawberries, raspberries, blackberries, blueberries, redcurrants and black cherries

75g/3oz/generous ⅓ cup caster (superfine) sugar

I tbsp cassis or Grand Marnier or orange juice

I Place the fruit into a medium saucepan, add the sugar, I tablespoon of water and the liqueur or orange juice and place over a medium heat, stirring gently occasionally. Allow the sugar to dissolve then bring the mixture to a gentle boil. Do not stir excessively, as this will cause the fruit to break up unnecessarily.

2 Store in a large Kilner jar in the fridge for up to I week and use as required.

LEMON CURD

My mother always made this lemon curd to put in a Swiss roll (jelly roll) instead of jam (see page 175). It is also delicious with other desserts or with breakfast pastries.

MAKES I JAR (V)

Finely grated zest and juice of 2 lemons

4 large eggs

150g/5oz/¾ cup caster (superfine) sugar

110g/4oz/I stick cold butter, cut into small cubes

I Put all the ingredients except the butter in a saucepan and using a hand whisk, whisk continuously over a very low heat until it thickens then slowly whisk in the butter, piece by piece, and cook, stirring all the time, for 10–12 minutes or until it thickens. At this stage the water should be on a very gentle simmer. When the curd is thick, transfer to sterilised jars, allow to cool and store in the fridge for up to I month.

LIST OF US COOKING TERMS

Here are some general American cooking terms which can be very useful, although there are often a few regional differences and variations.

UK	US	UK	US
almonds (flaked)	almonds (slivered)	kitchen paper	paper towels
aubergine	eggplant	langoustines	Norway lobster
baking beans	pie weights	lettuce leaves	salad greens
barbecue	grill	Little Gem lettuce	Boston lettuce
beetroot	beet	main course	entrée
bicarbonate of soda	baking soda	mangetout	snow peas
biscuit	cookie	minced (meat)	ground
black pudding	blood sausage	muslin	cheesecloth
button mushrooms	white mushrooms	Parma ham	prosciutto
cake mixture	cake batter	(shortcrust)	pie dough
caster sugar	superfine sugar	pastry case	pastry shell
celeriac	celery root	pepper (sweet)	bell pepper
clingfilm	plastic wrap	piping bag	pastry bag
cocktail stick	toothpick	plain flour	all-purpose flour
coriander (fresh)	cilantro	porridge oats	oatmeal
cornflour	cornstarch	poussin	squab chicken
Cos lettuce	Romaine lettuce	prawns	shrimp
courgette	zucchini	pudding basin	ovenproof bowl
demerara sugar	raw brown sugar	rashers	slices
double cream	heavy cream	self-raising flour	self-rising flour
fillet (beef, pork)	tenderloin	sieve	strainer
filo pastry	phyllo pastry	spring onion	scallion
flan dish	tart pan	starter	appetizer
floury (potatoes)	mealy	stone	pit
fresh root ginger	gingerroot	sultanas	golden raisins
French beans	green beans	sweetcorn	corn
fridge	refrigerator	Swiss roll	jelly roll
ginger nuts	gingersnaps	tea towel	dishtowel
glacé cherries	candied cherries	tiger prawns	jumbo shrimp
golden syrup	corn syrup	tin (roasting tin, loaf tin)	pan
griddle pan	grill pan	tin	can
grill	broiler	tomato purée	tomato paste
icing	frosting	vanilla pod	vanilla bean
icing sugar	confectioner's sugar	wholemeal flour	wholewheat flour
jam	jelly	wire rack	cooling rack
jug	pitcher	work surface	counter
kebab	kabob	yoghurt (natural)	yogurt (plain)

INDEX

ACKNOWLEDGEMENTS

Recipes that Work has worked because of the wonderful assistance I have received in its compilation.

I would like to thank my wife Catherine for all of her input and feedback in relation to the book.

Sincere thanks to Edward Hayden for his continued commitment and dedication to this and our many other projects.

Special mention to Martine Carter who keeps me on the 'straight and narrow'!

Thanks also to Helen Donnelly who assisted in the recipe trials.

To Sophie Martin, Martin Poole, Caroline Curtis and Felicity Barnum-Bobb for helping to make the dream a reality.

I would like to thank the team at HarperCollins: Jenny Heller, Ione Walder, Elen Jones, Moira Reilly, Oliver Goodwin, Kathy Dyke and Georgina Atsiaris for all their commitment and dedication.